BRAIN GAMES®

EXTREME

DOT-TO-DOT

Publications International, Ltd.

Allison Wong

Puzzle source images: Shutterstock.com

Louis Weber, CEO

Publications International, Ltd.

7373 North Cicero Avenue

Lincolnwood, Illinois 60712

Permission is never granted for commercial purposes.

ISBN: 978-1-68022-314-9

Manufactured in China.

8 7 6 5 4 3 2 1

Brain Games is a registered trademark of Publications International, Ltd.

RELAX AND . . . CONNECT

Sharpen your pencils and rev up your fine motor skills! These puzzles are big enough to keep you connecting dots for those pleasant stretches of time when you just want to unwind, but still do something. They're intricate (at times devious!) and are constructed in a way to keep you engaged and curious as the picture reveals itself.

Look for dot number 1 and begin connecting the dots in numeric order. You may want to use a pencil in case you need to erase and straighten a line. For long lines, use a ruler to keep them straight. For the really crowded sections you may want to use a magnifying glass! You can also look at completed pictures in the answer key at the back of the book.

We've picked a variety of images, so there's no telling what the connected dots will reveal. The titles might give you a bit of a hint—but they won't give the subject away. And if you're a colorist, you'll also enjoy giving the completed pictures some color and shading!

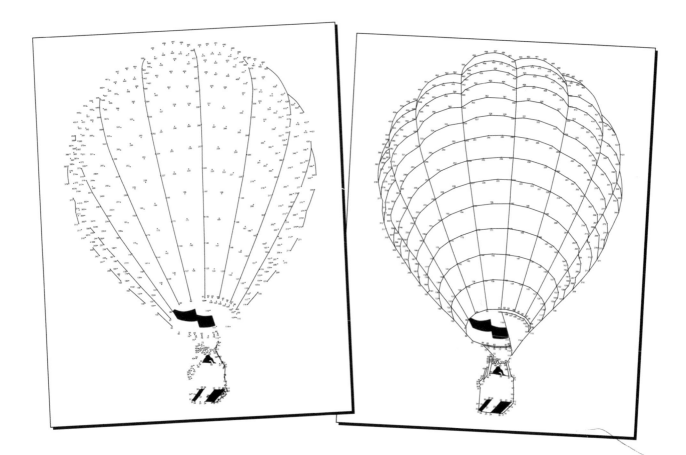

I'm Not Crabby!

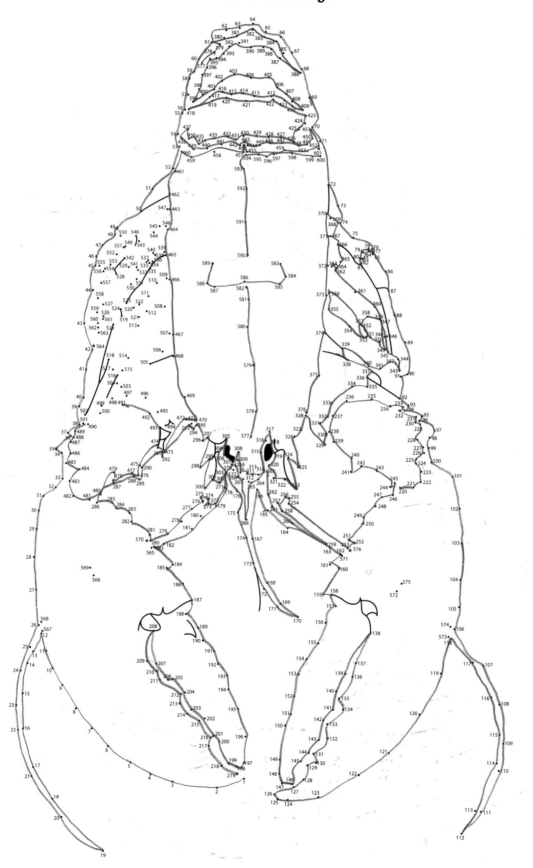

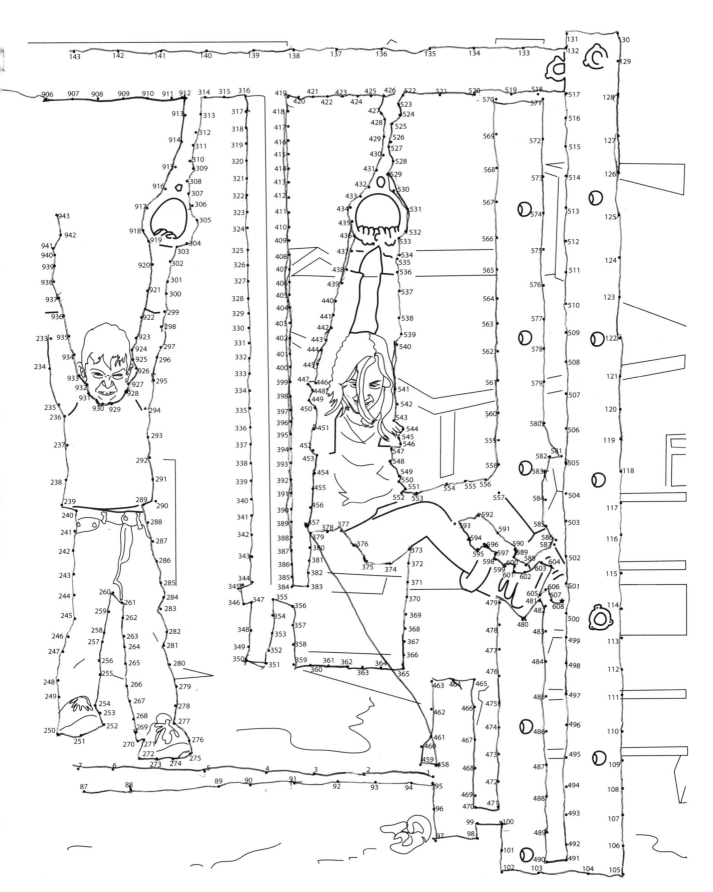

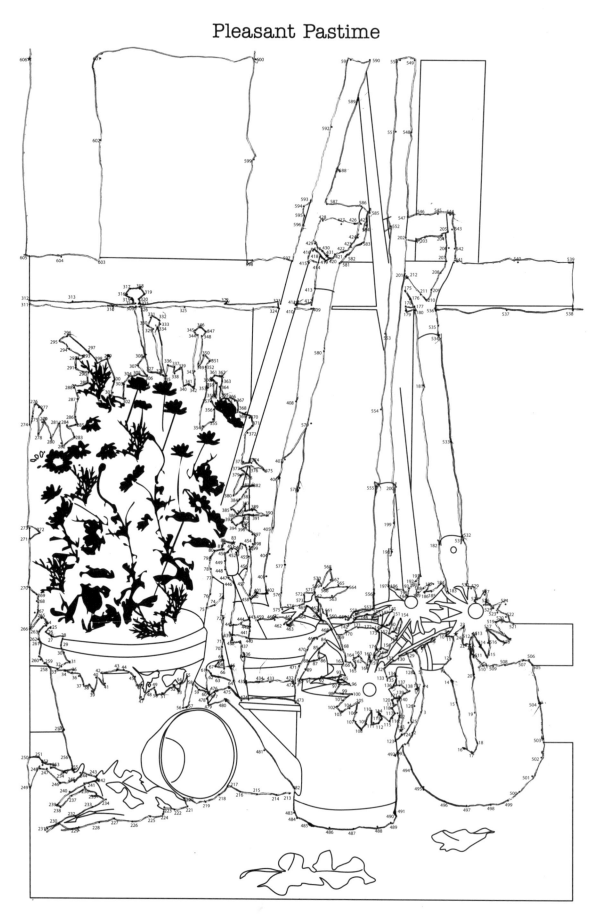

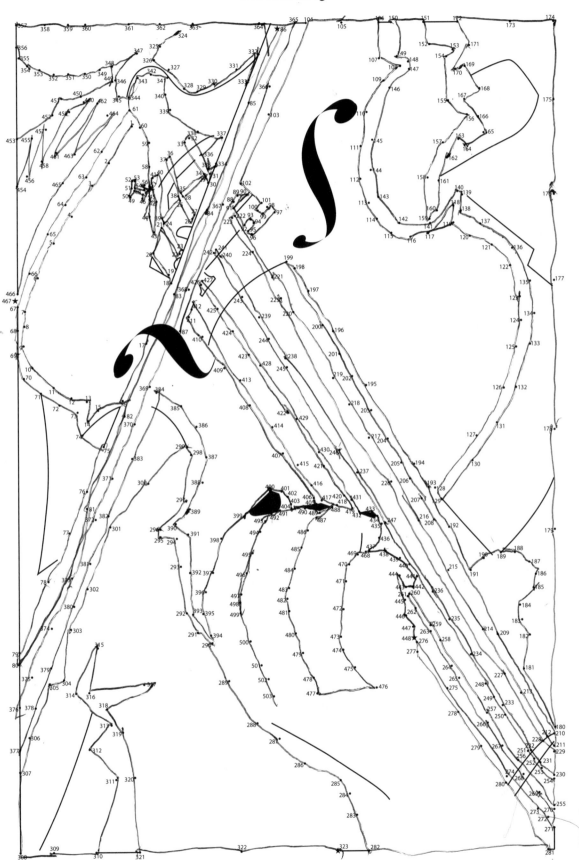

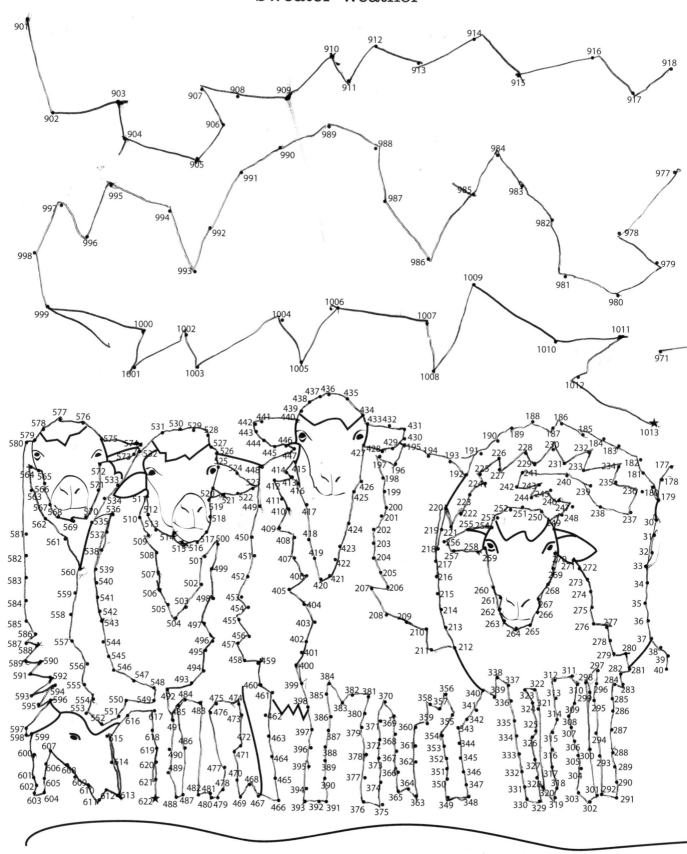

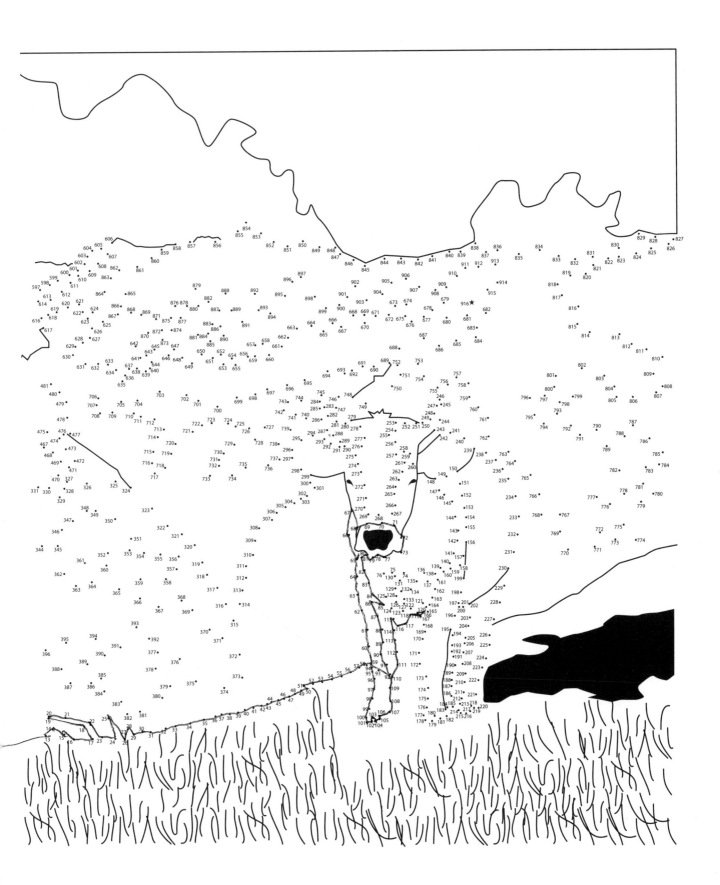

17

Icy Resolve

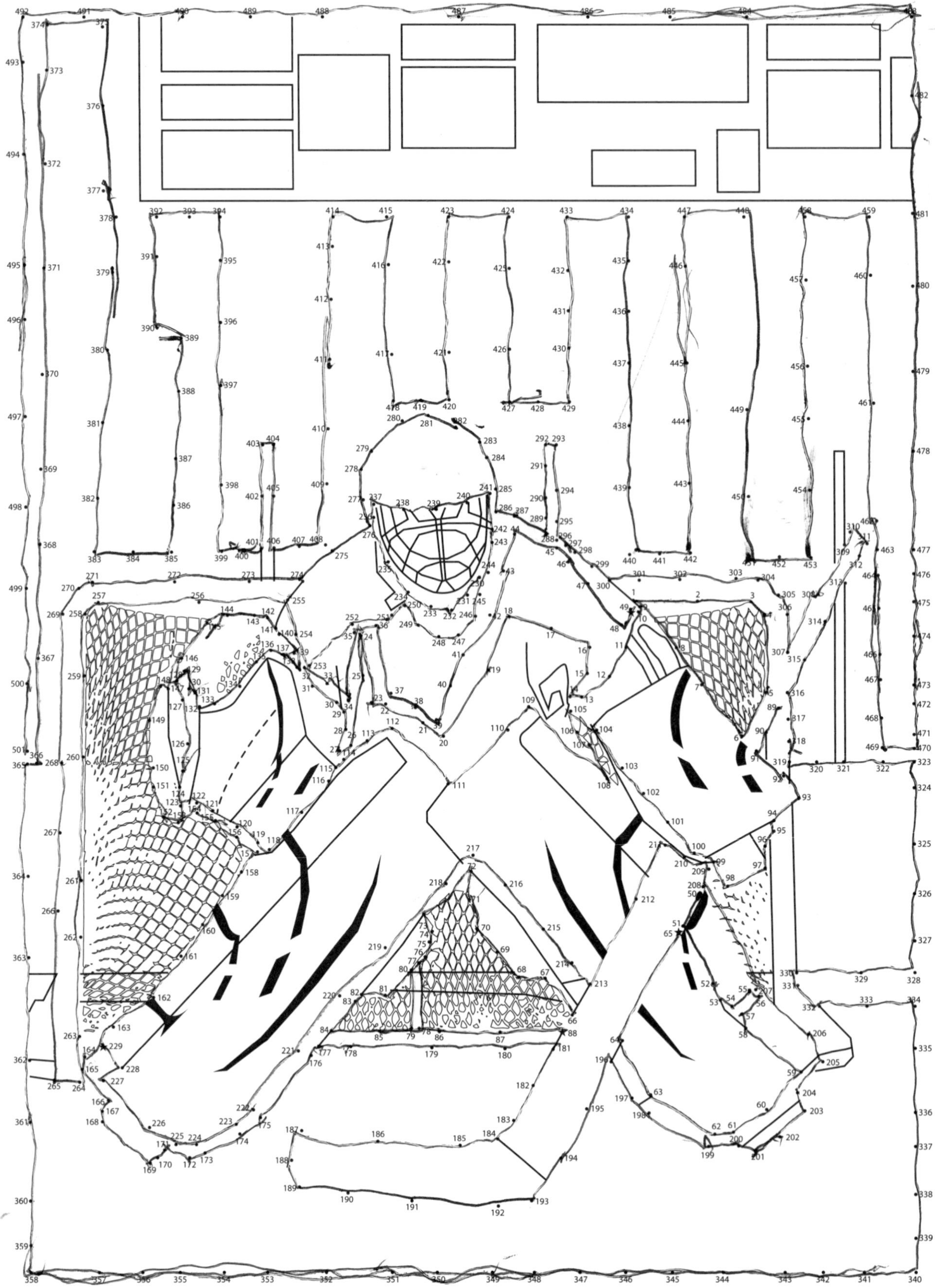

Go Time

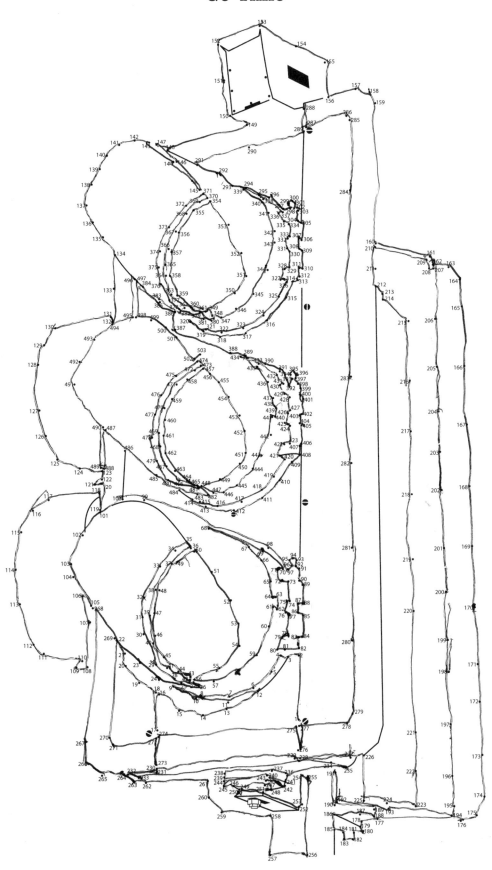

19

Polar Opposites

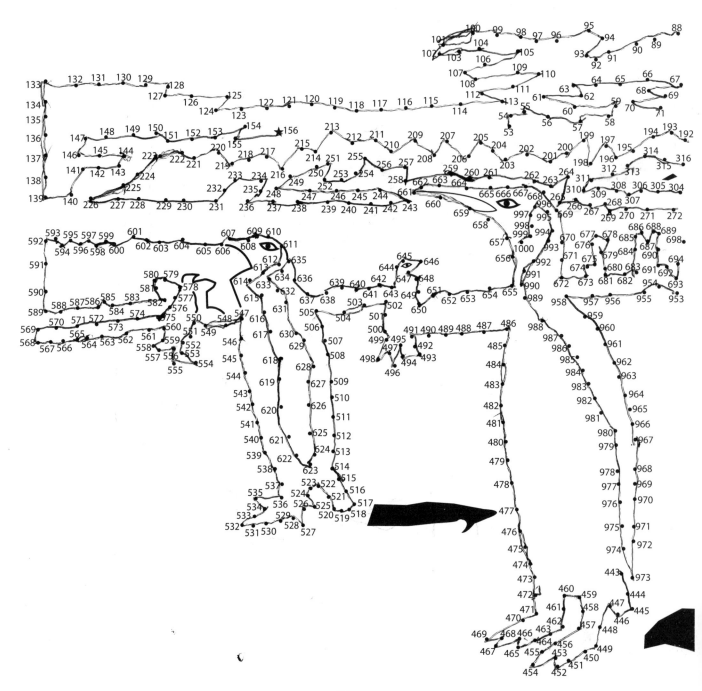

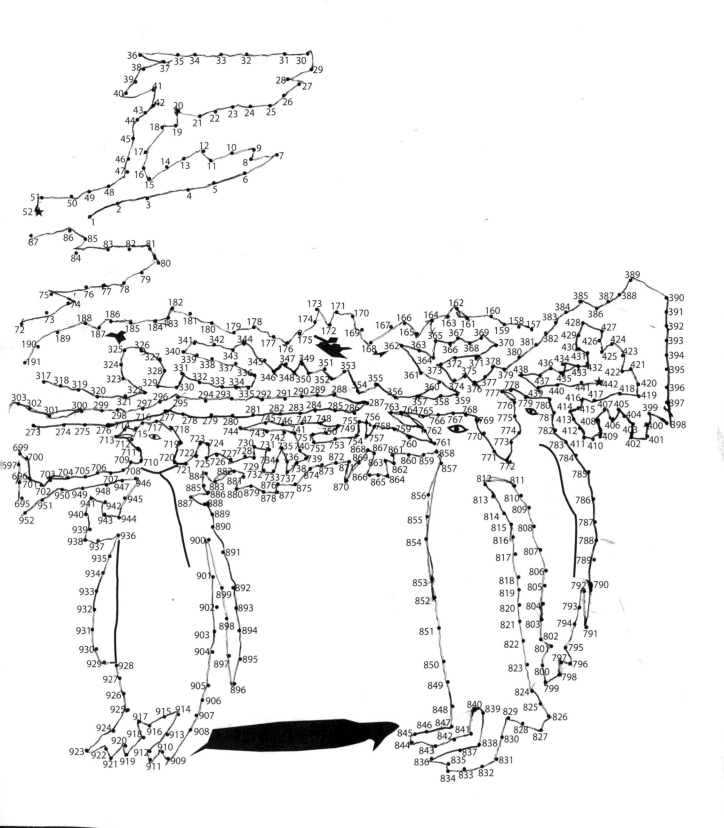

Fenced In

A Masquerade

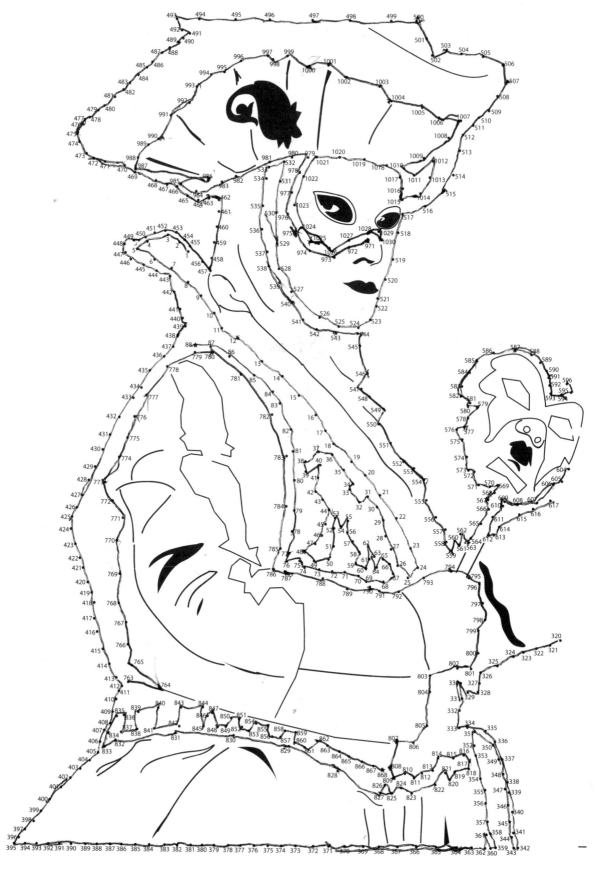

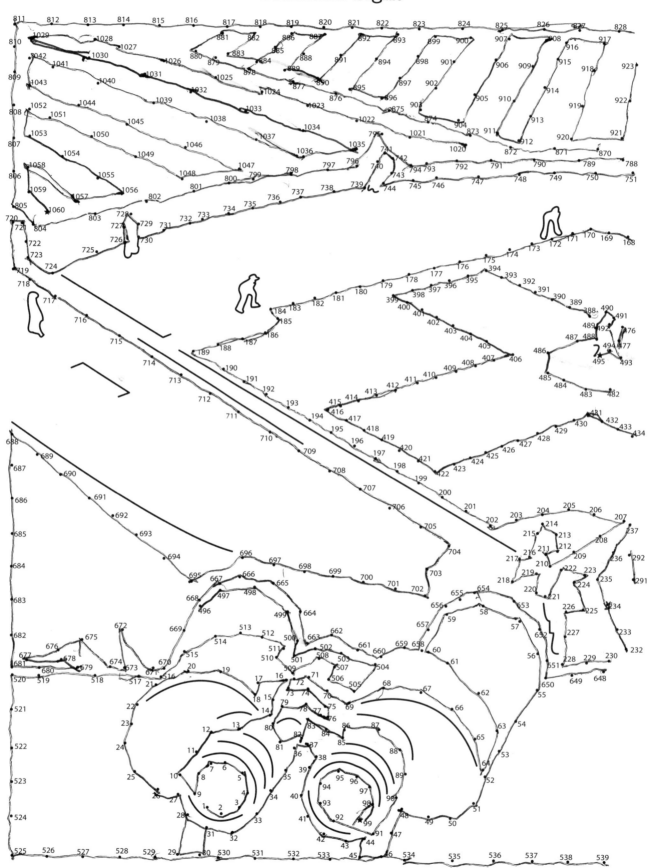

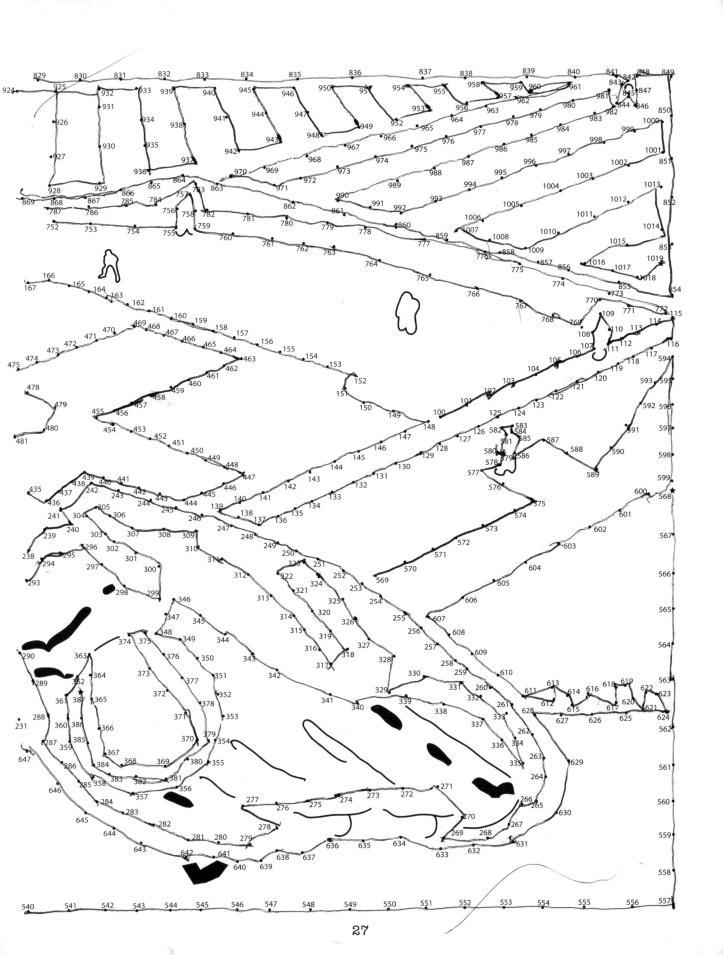

27

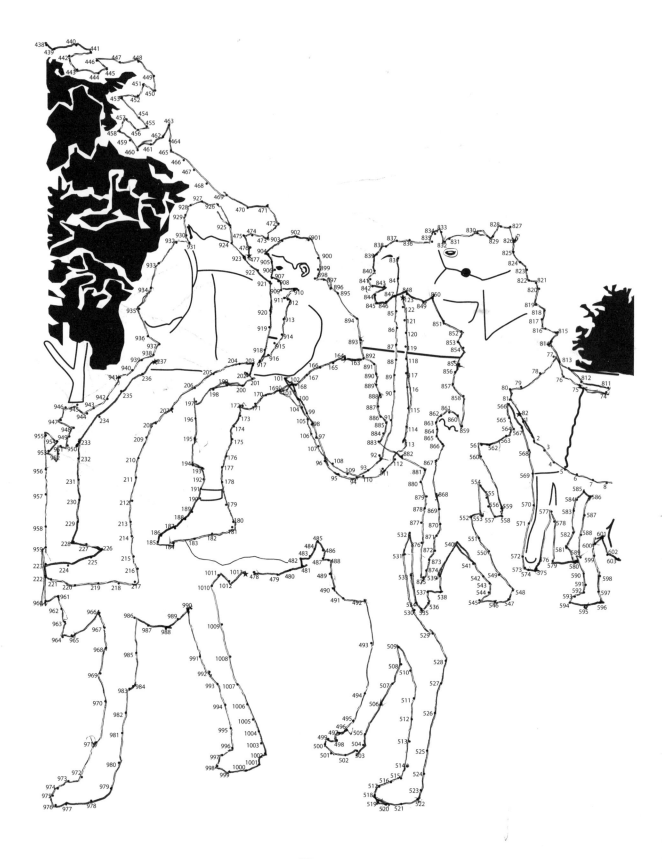

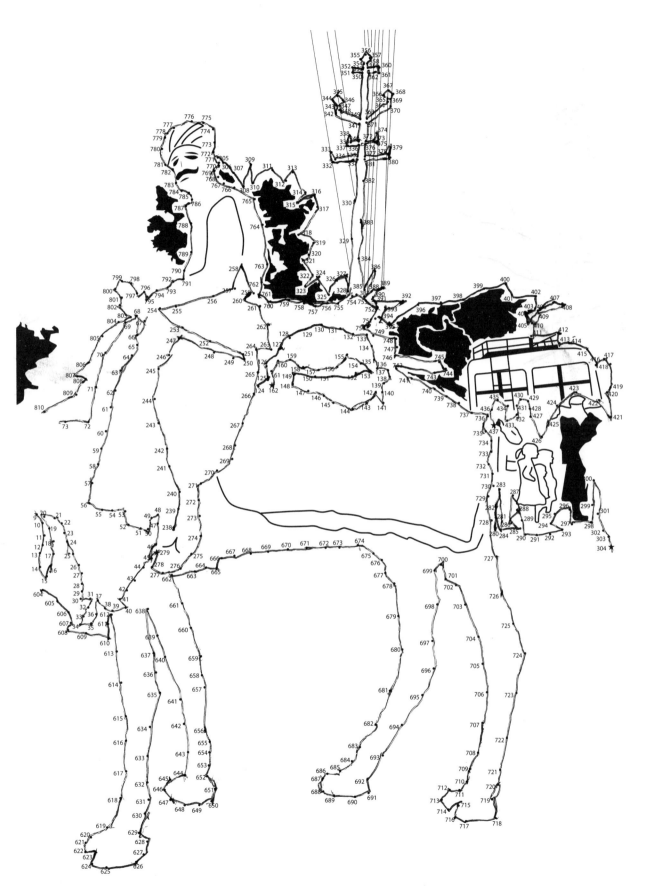

29

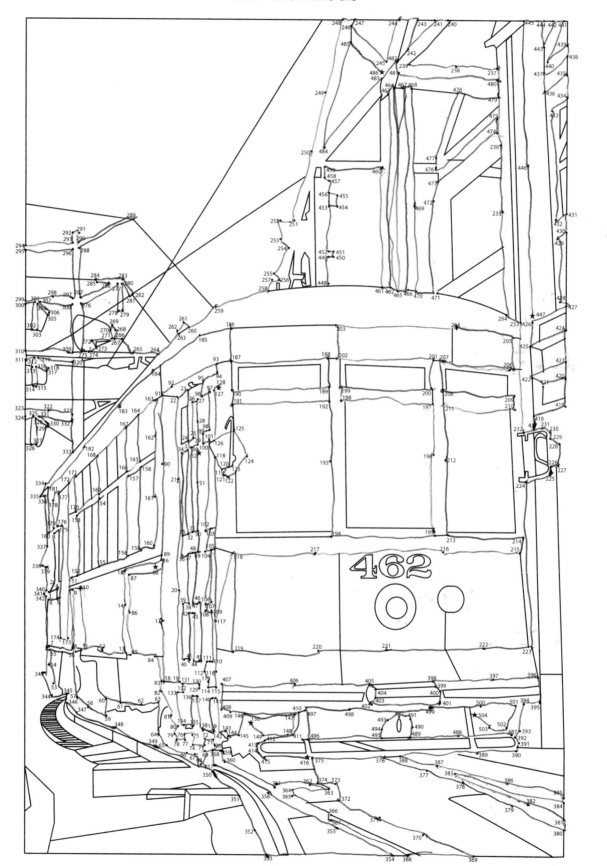

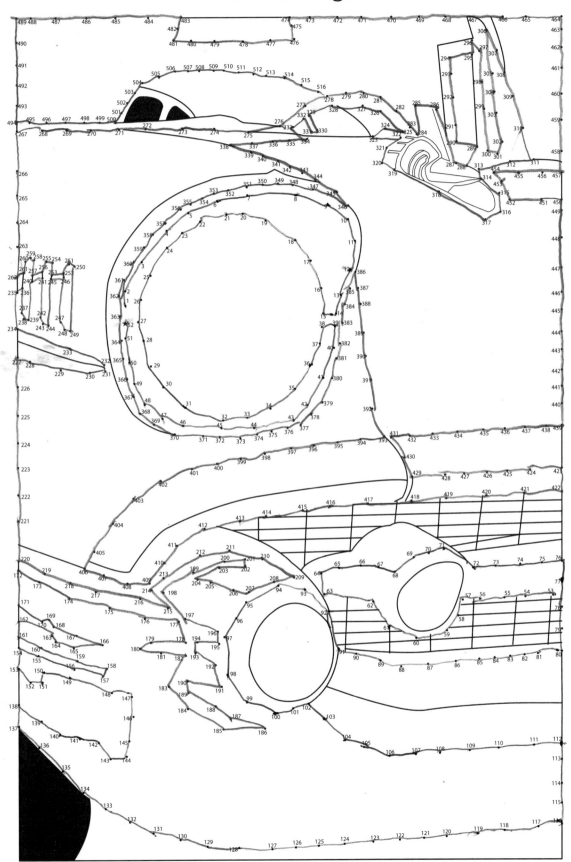

Frozen in Place

33

Perfect Perch

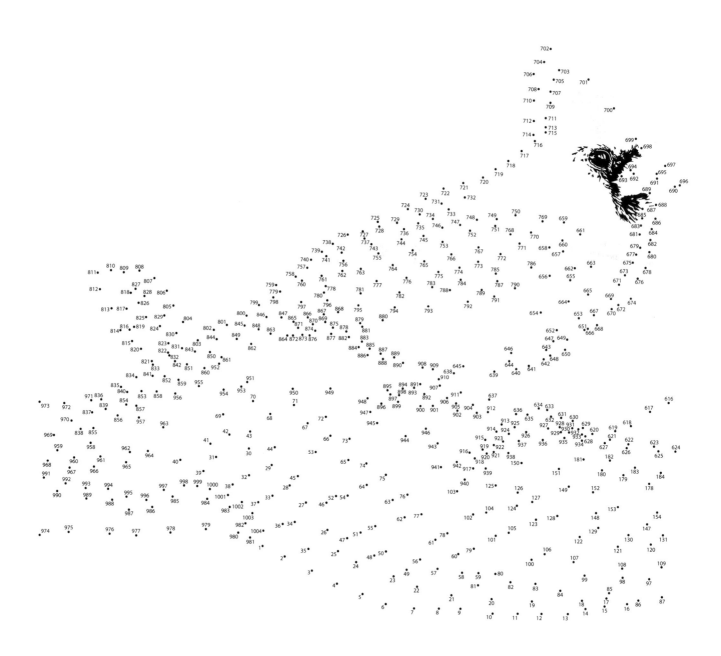

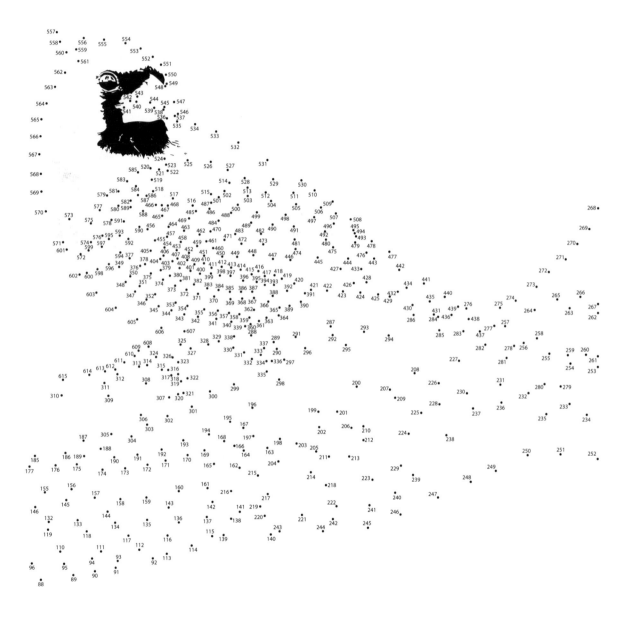

A Good Return

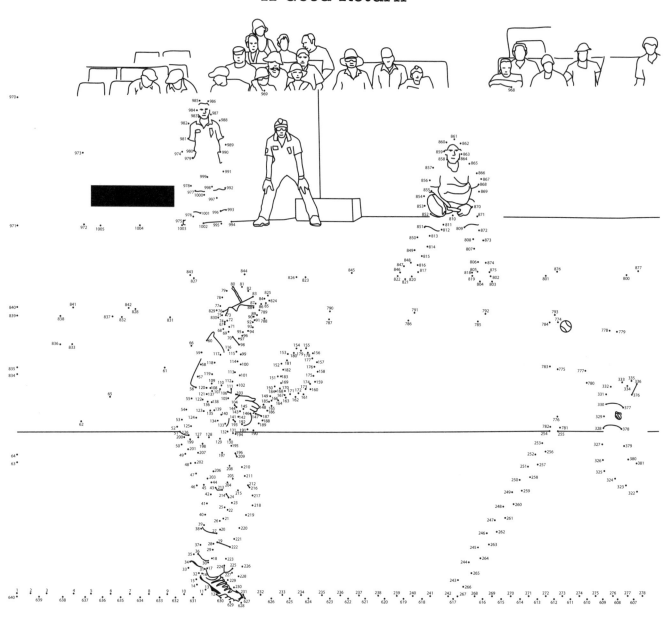

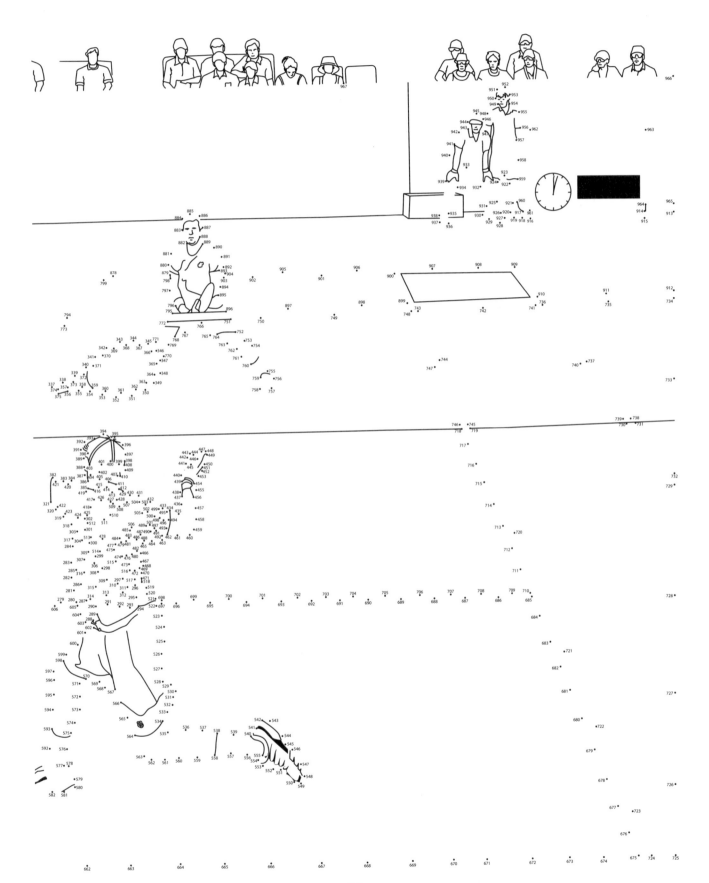

40

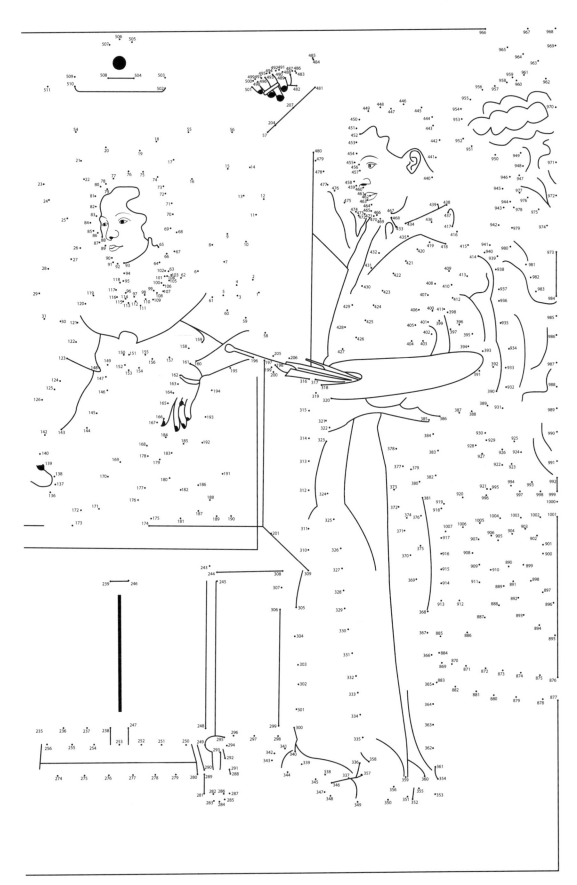

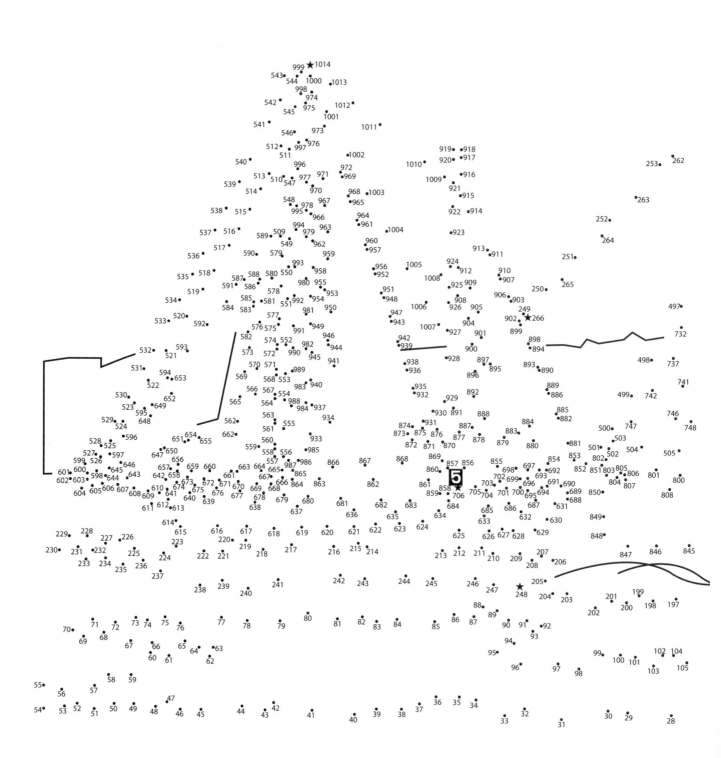

And Then She Said . . .

44

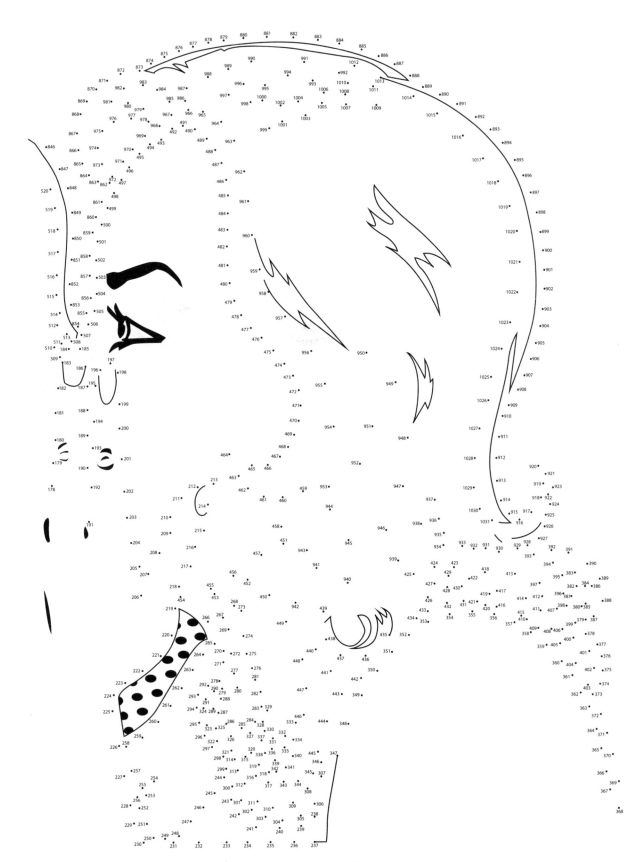

45

Hay, But Not a Loft

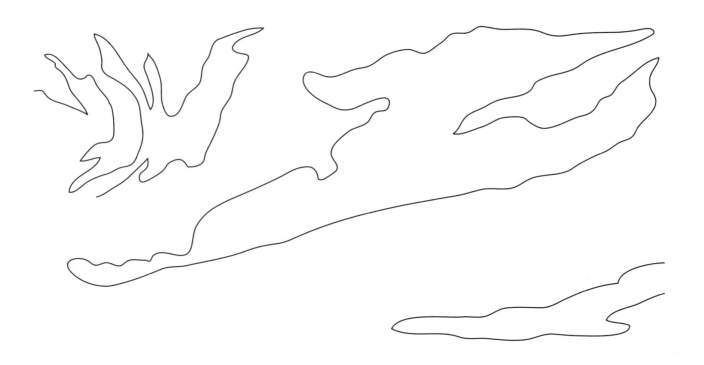

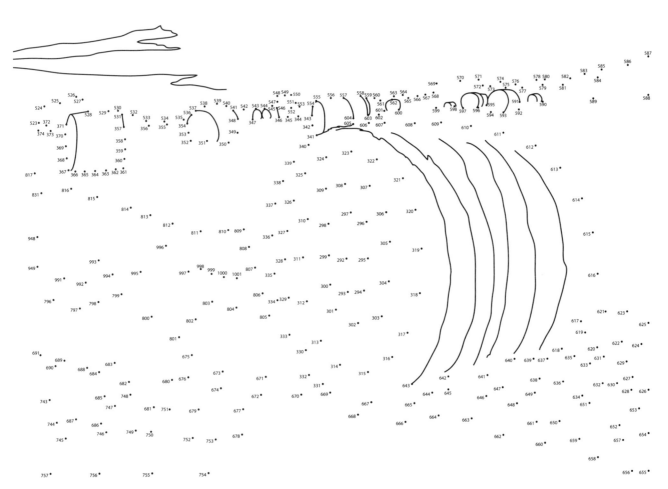

Fruit of the Land

49

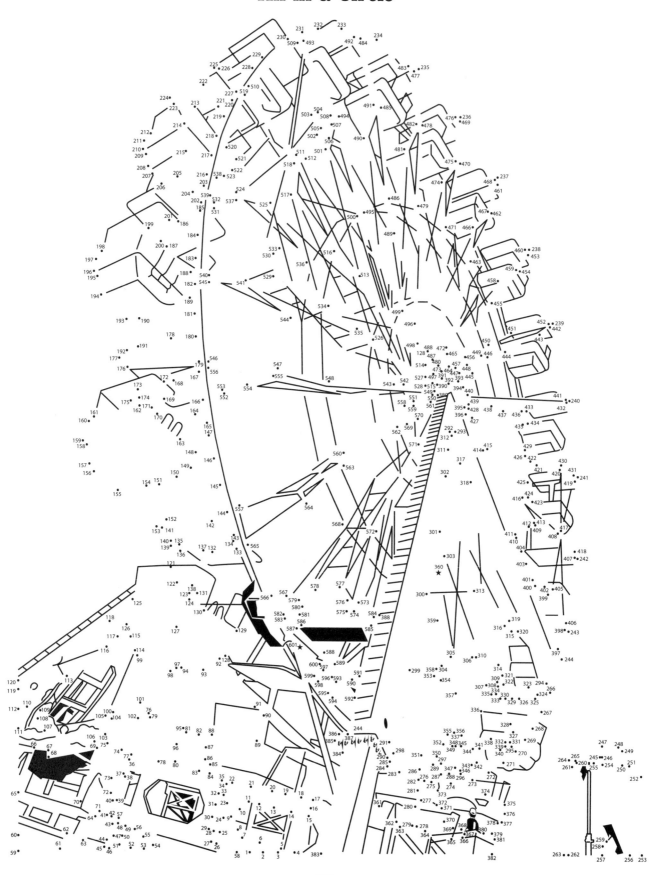

Nectar for Royalty

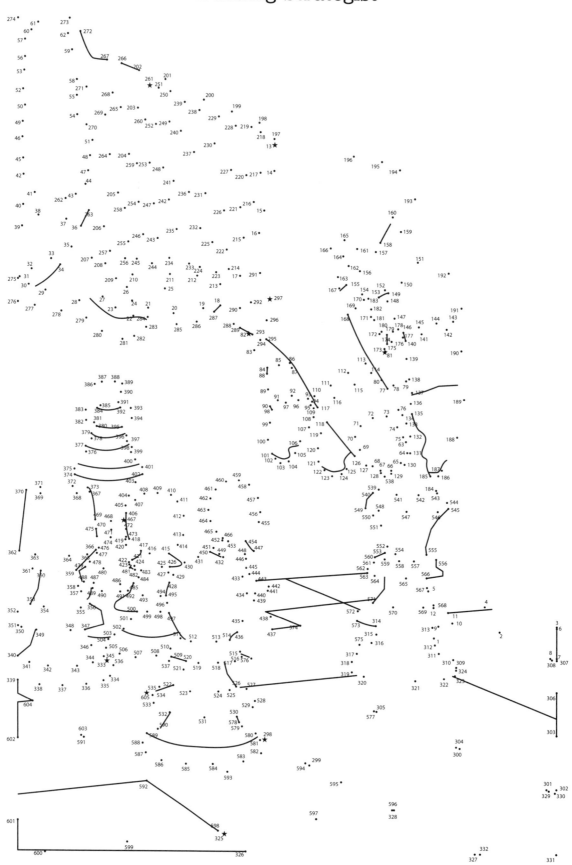

Prance and Bob

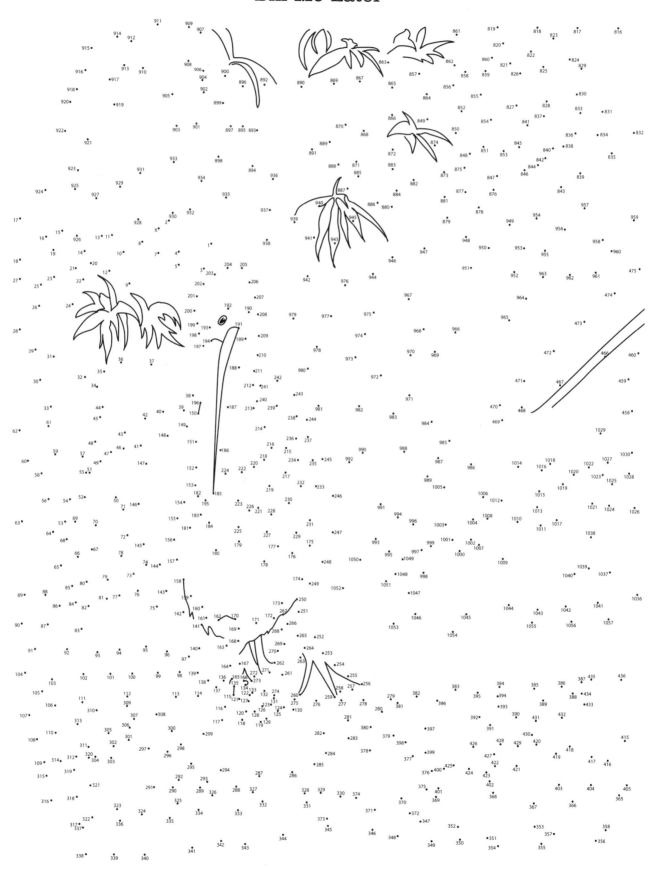

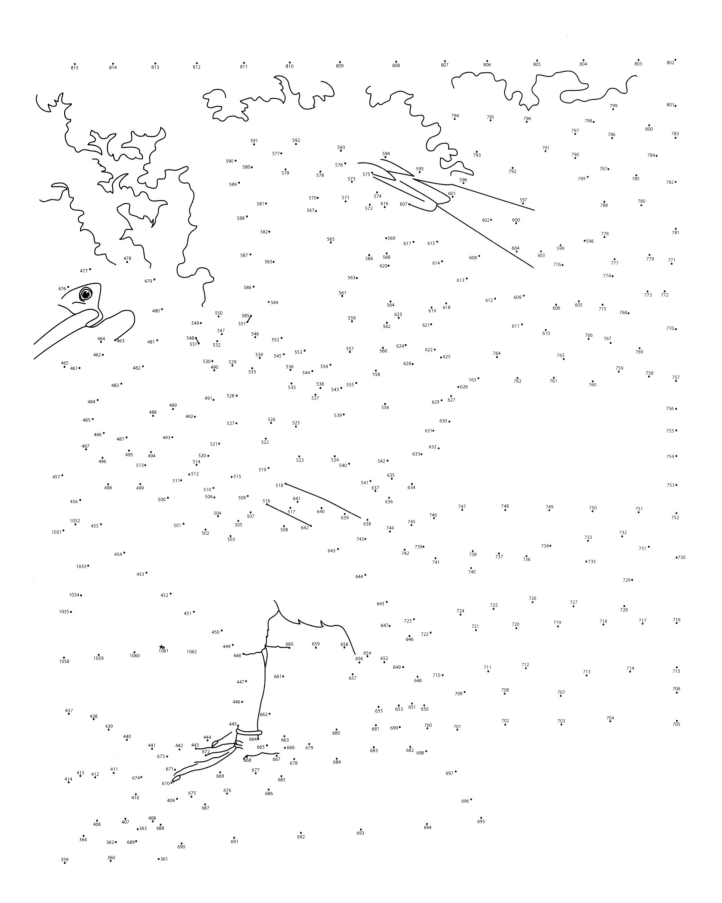

Implacability

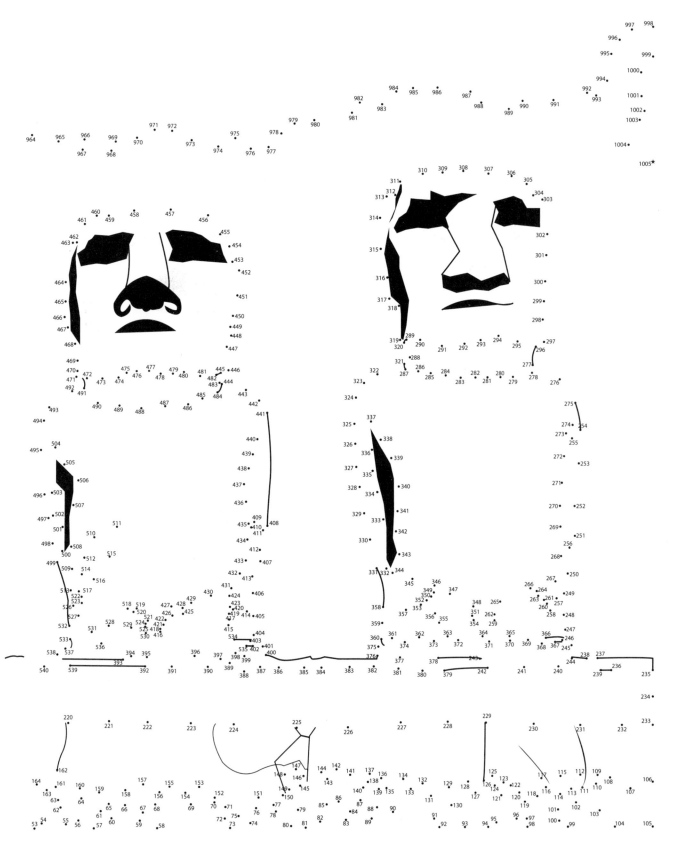

61

Cap It Off

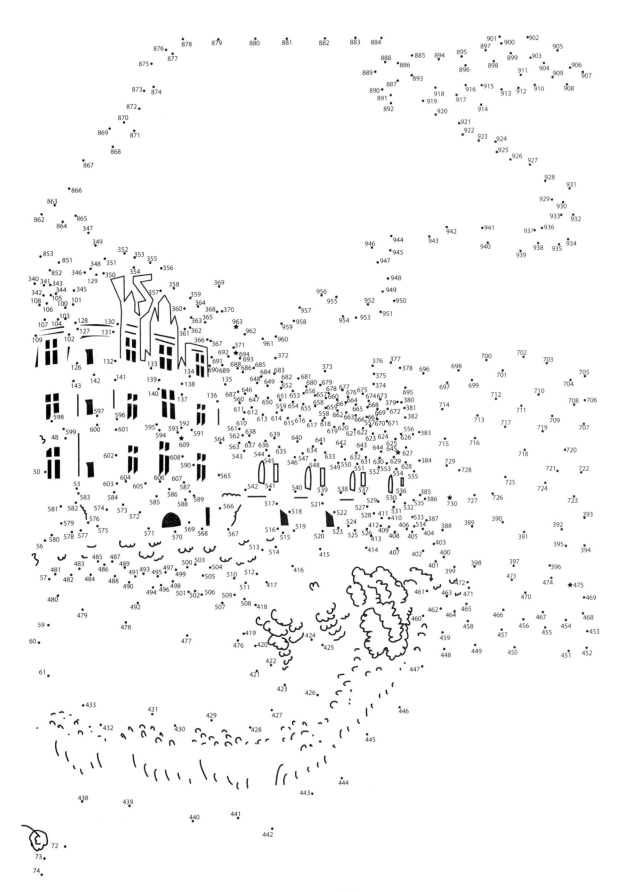

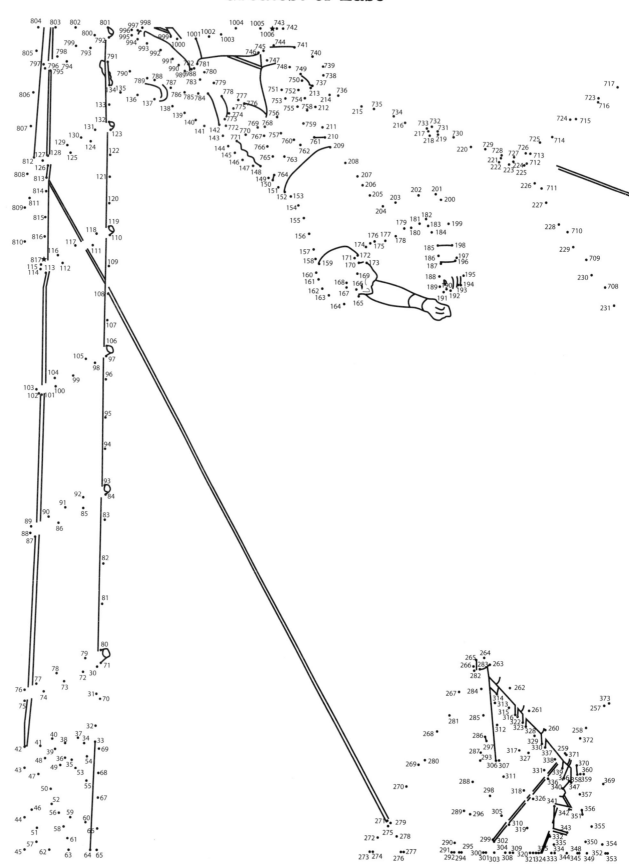

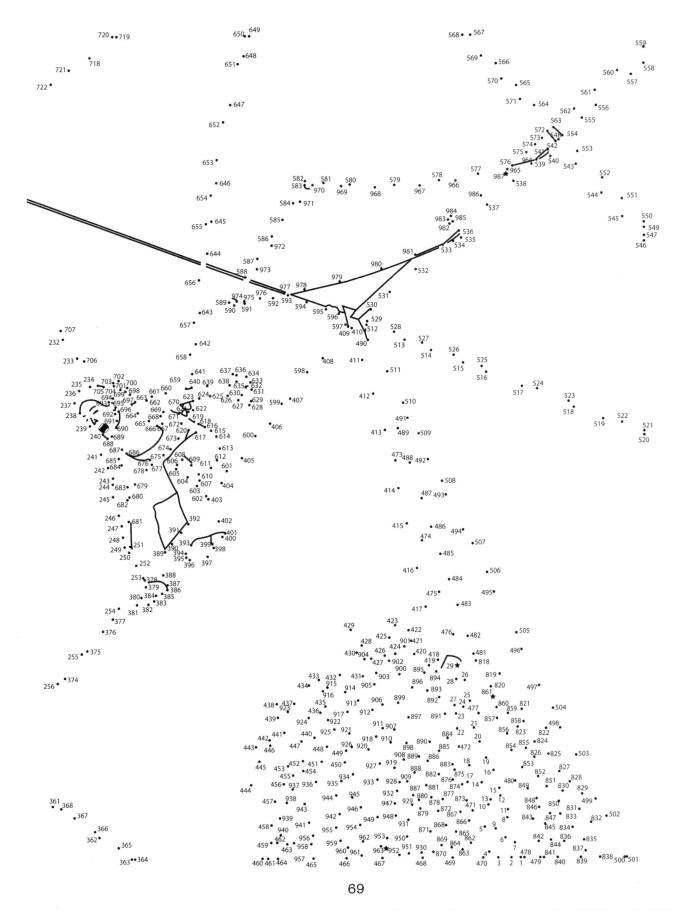

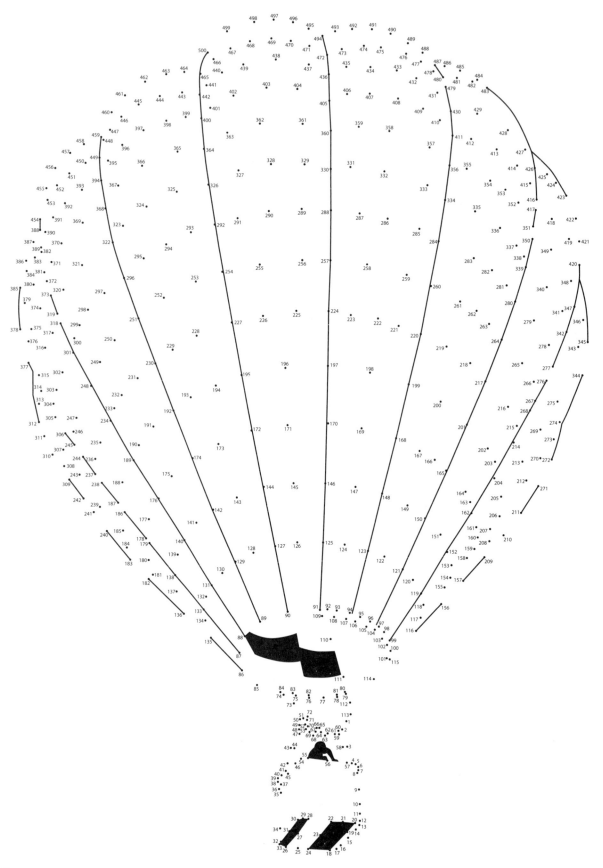

Simple Repast

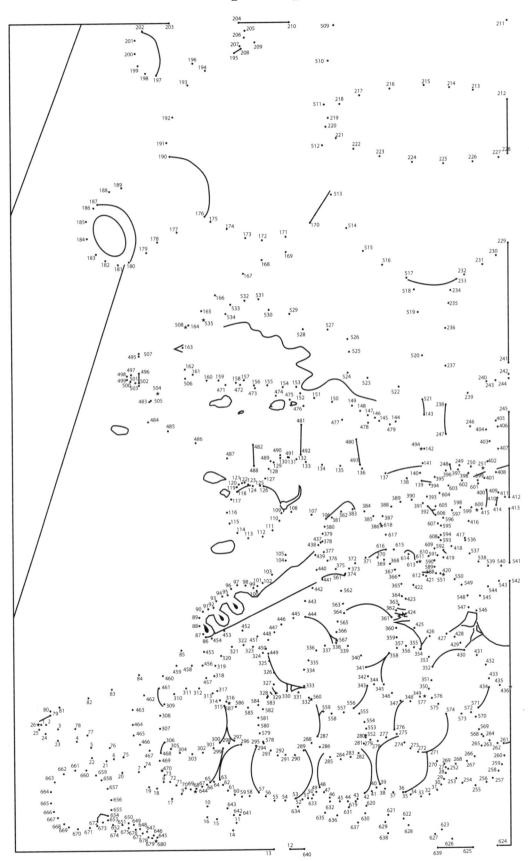

71

It's a Stretch

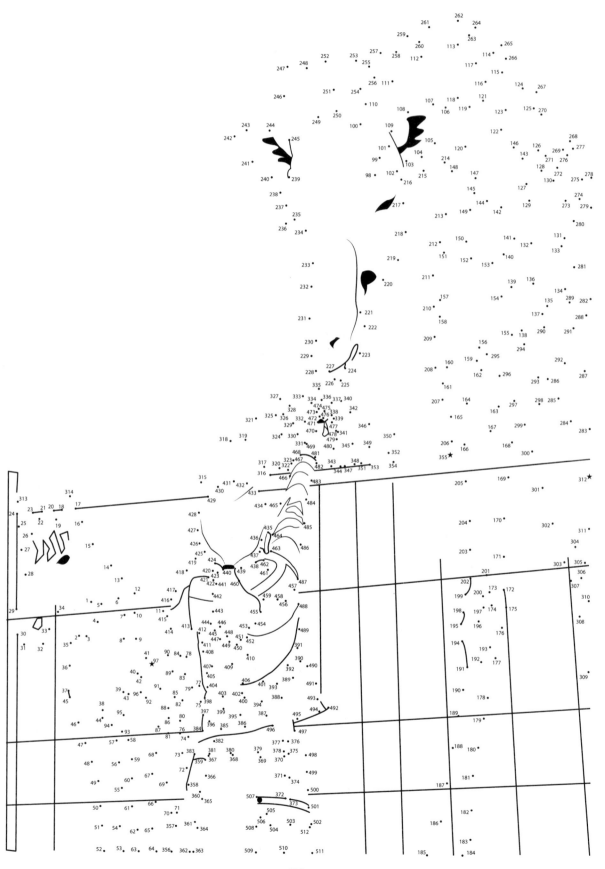

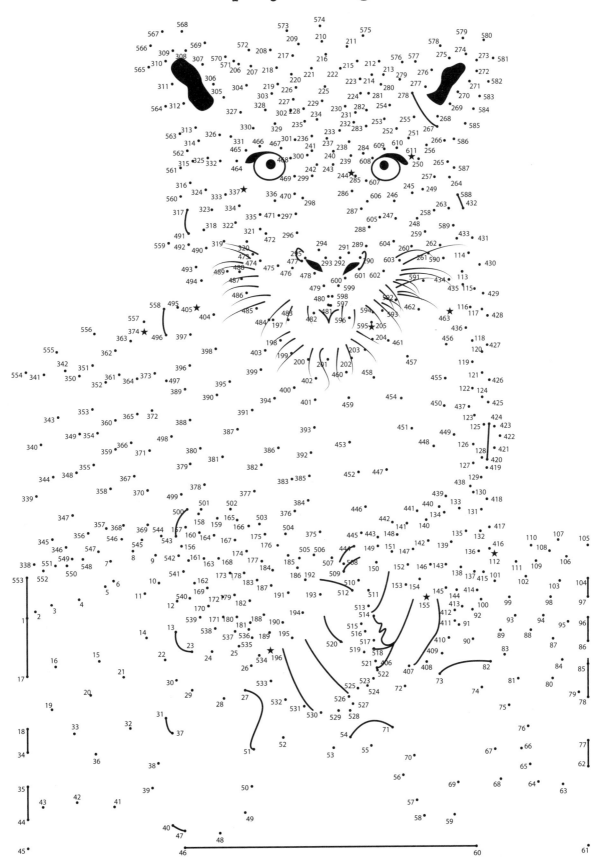

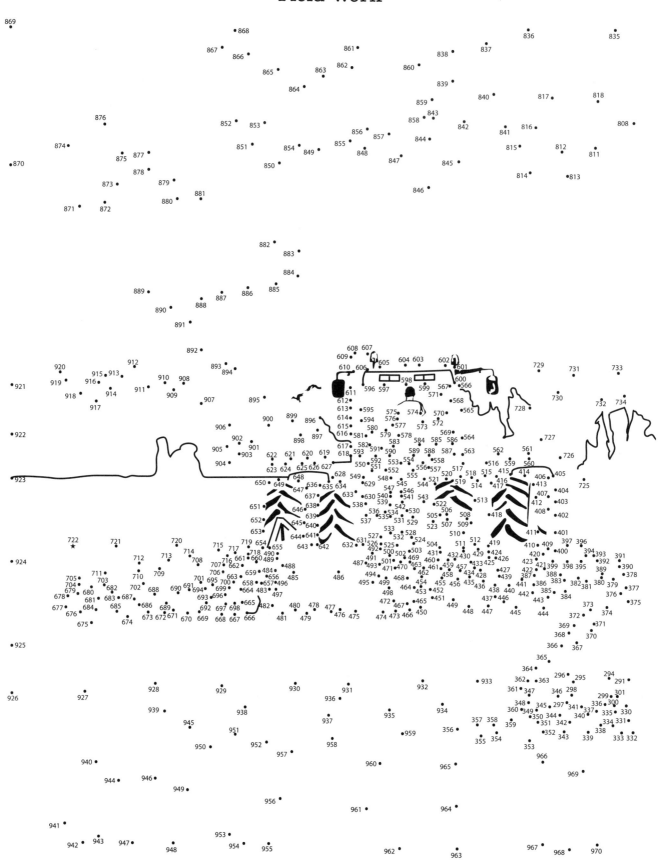

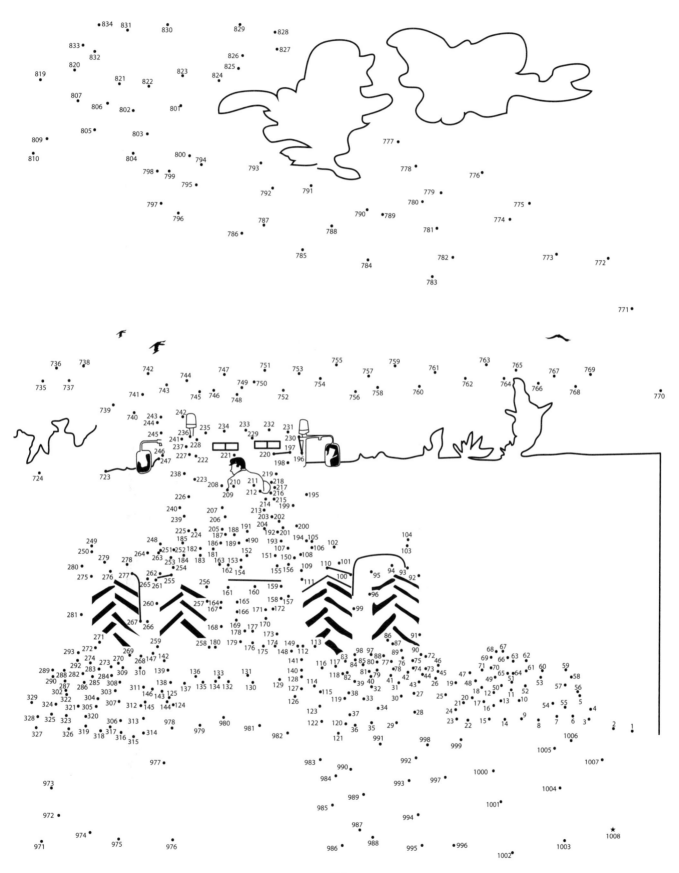

Large Portion

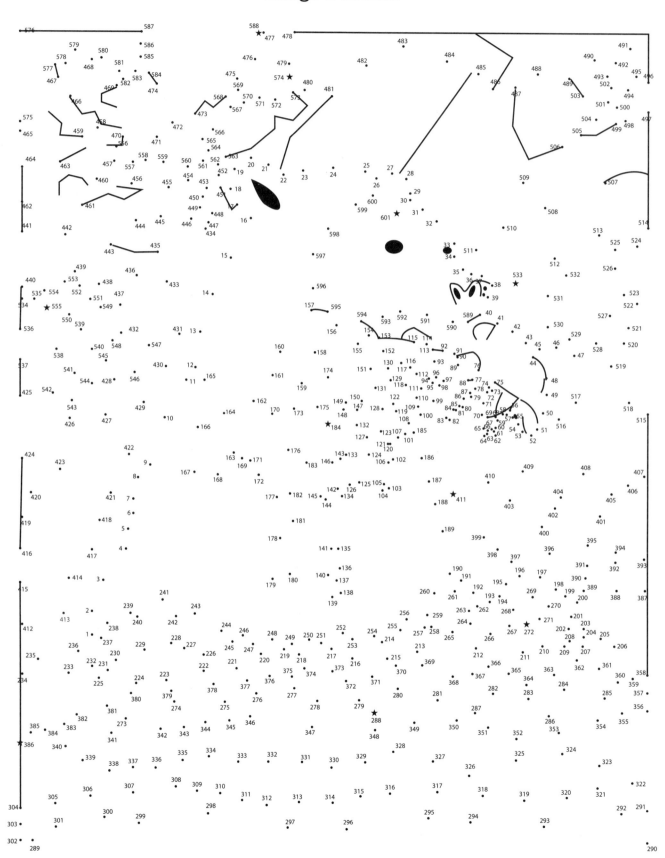

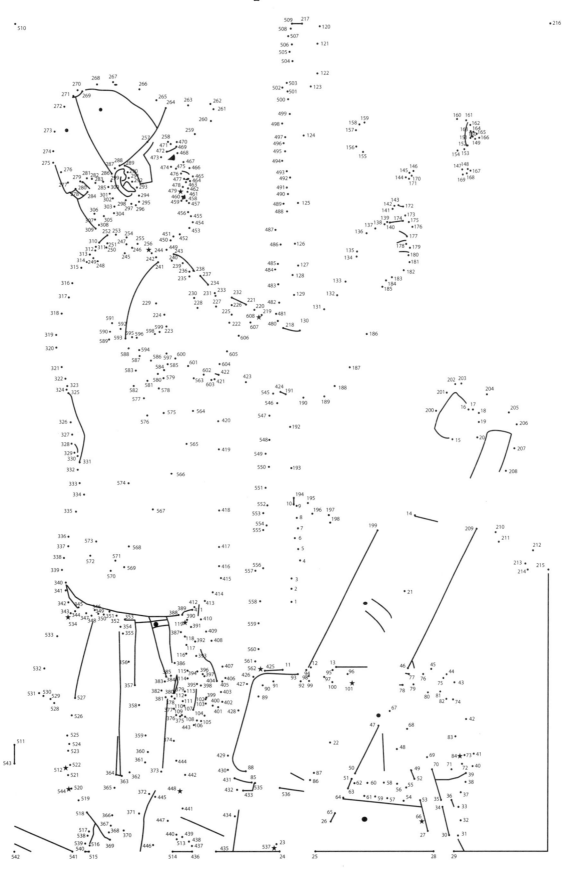

Feeling Winded

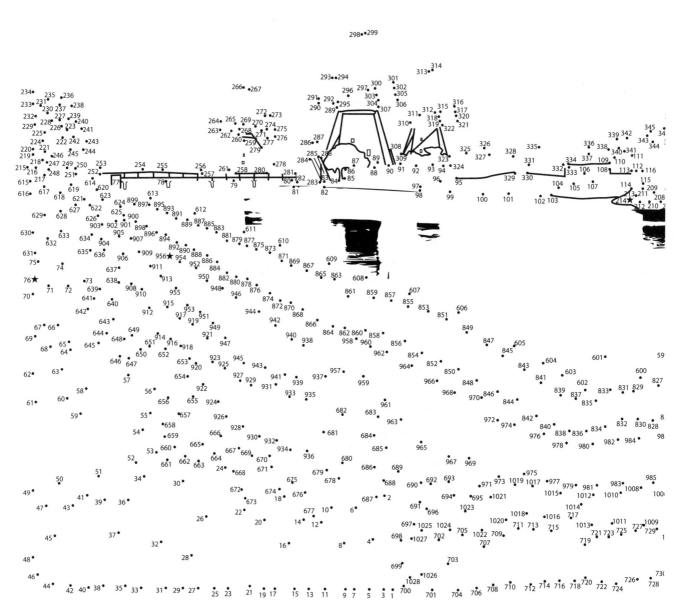

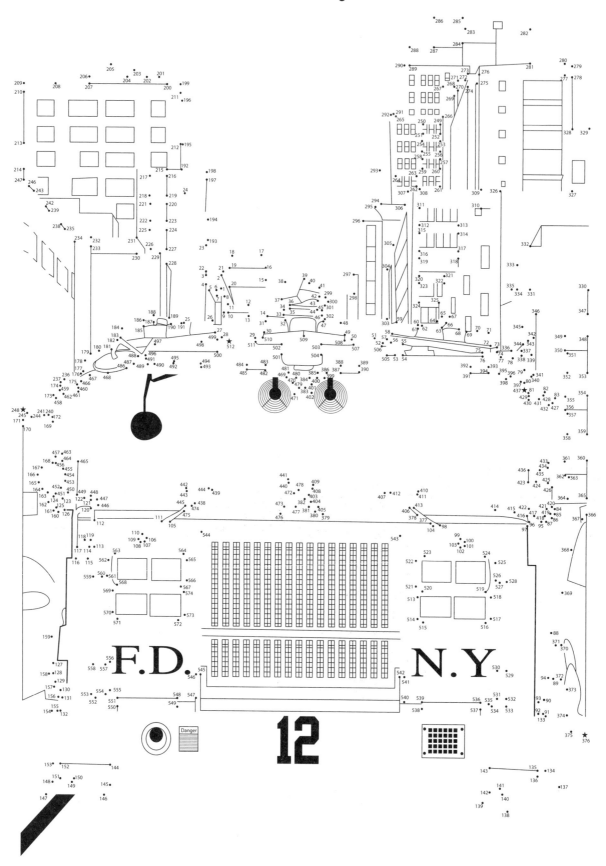

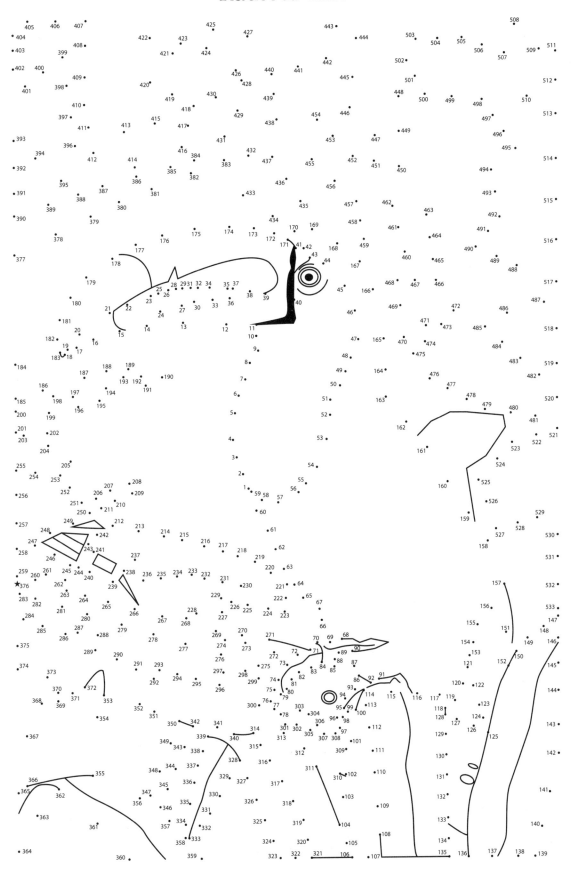

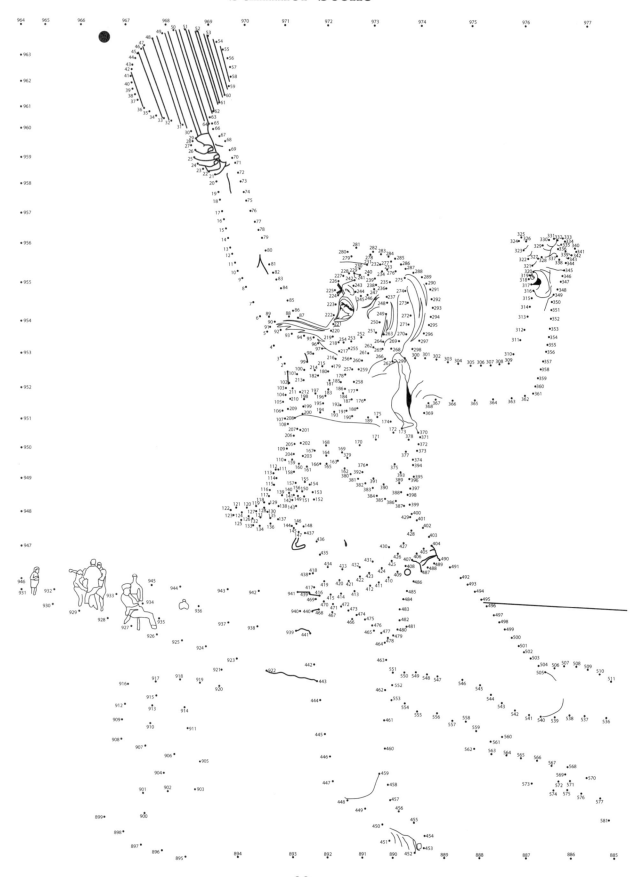

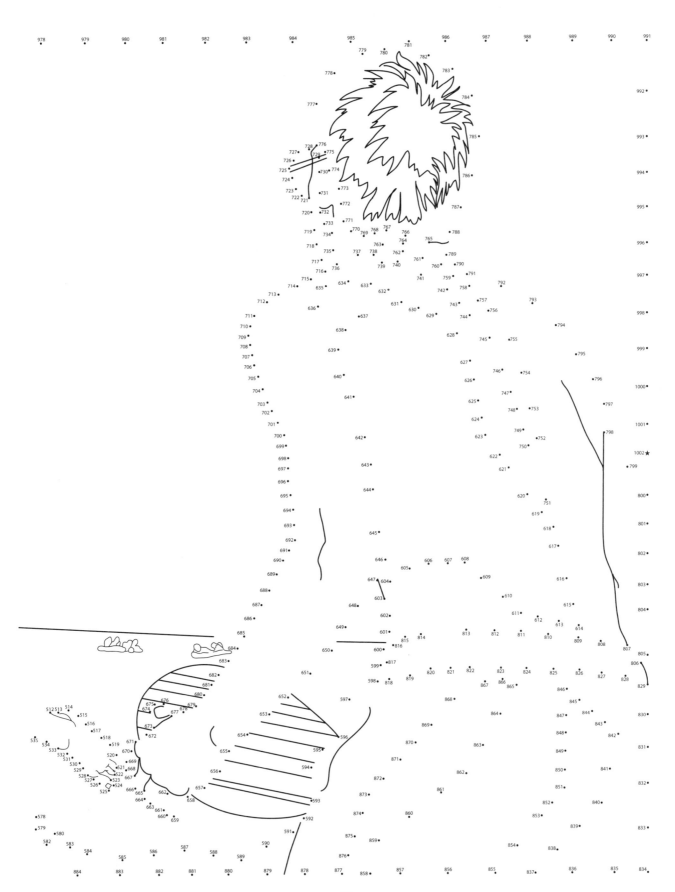

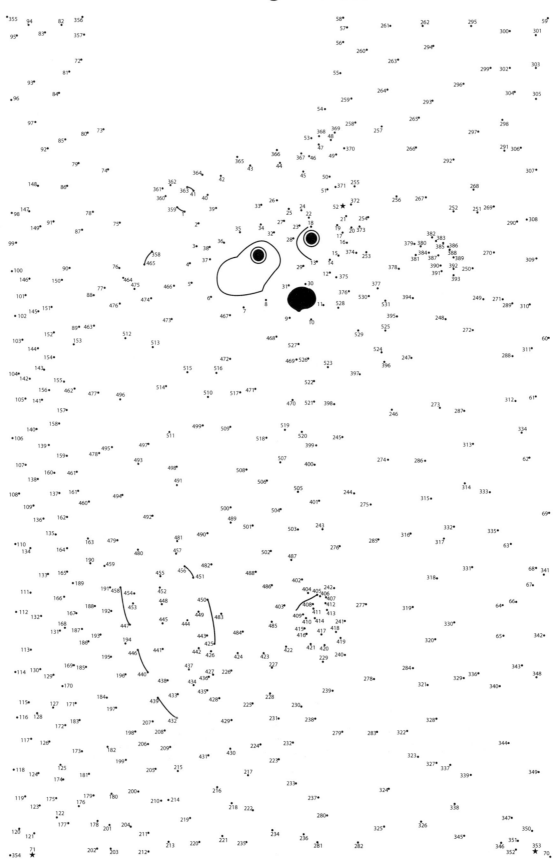

City Scene

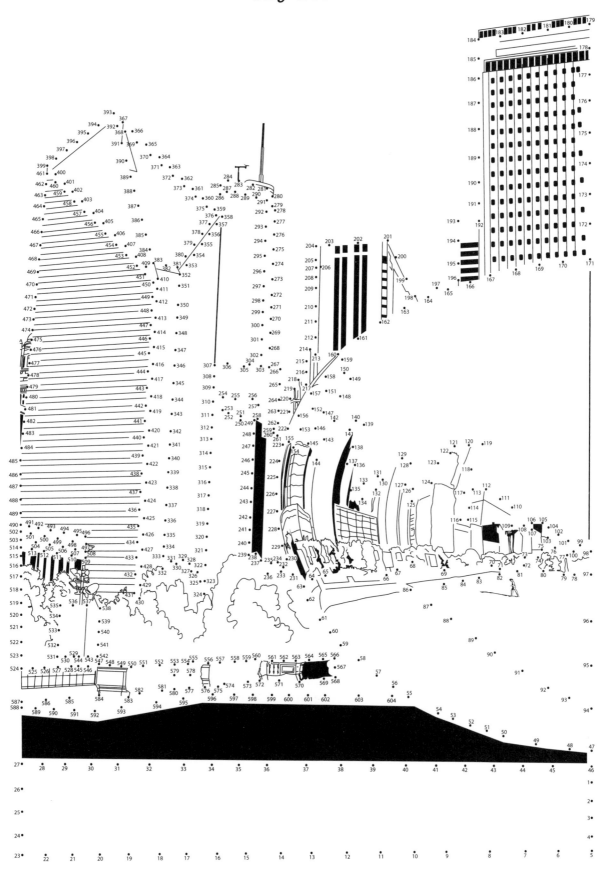

93

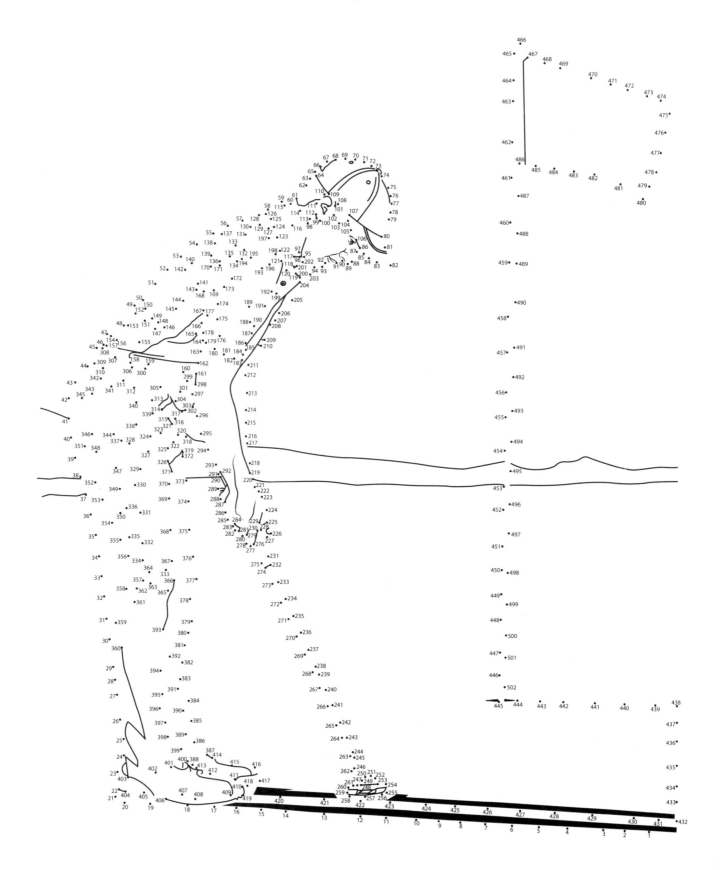

Hang Loose

95

Wigging Out

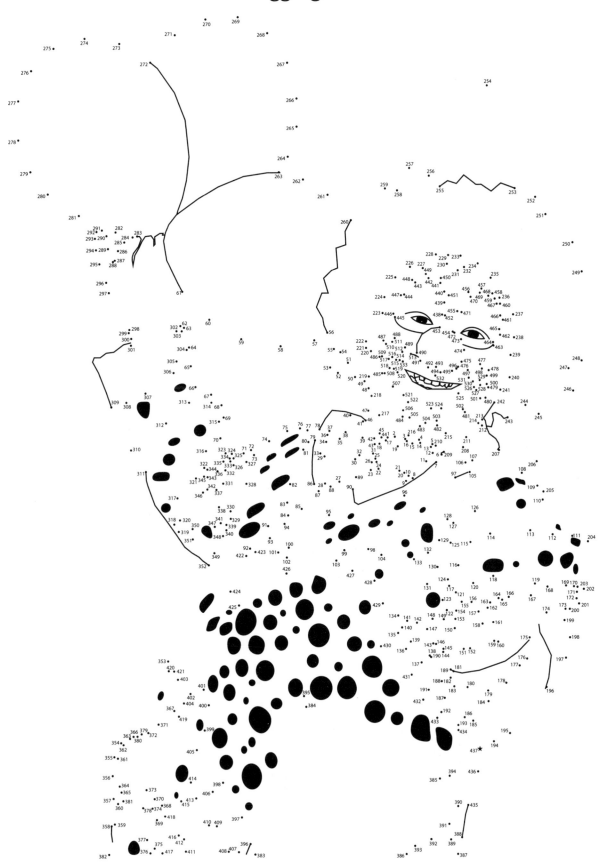

Did It!

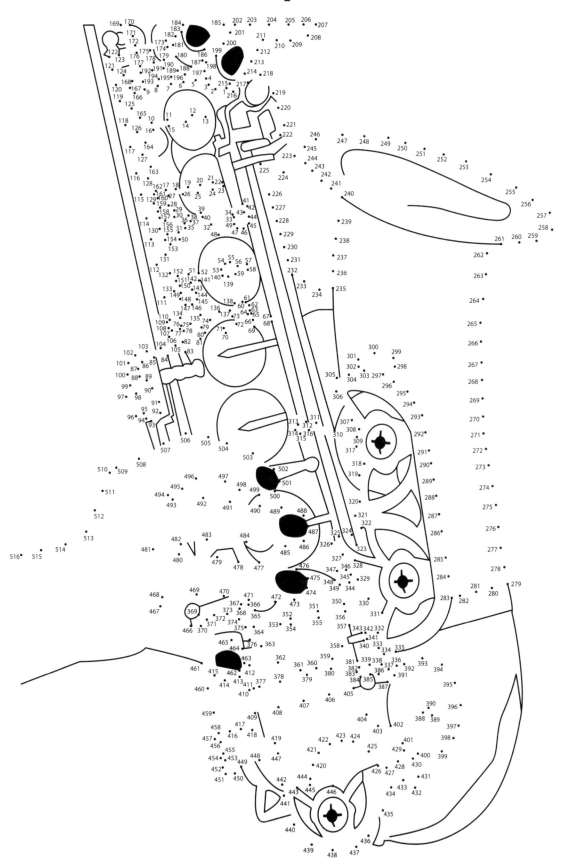

Like Swans

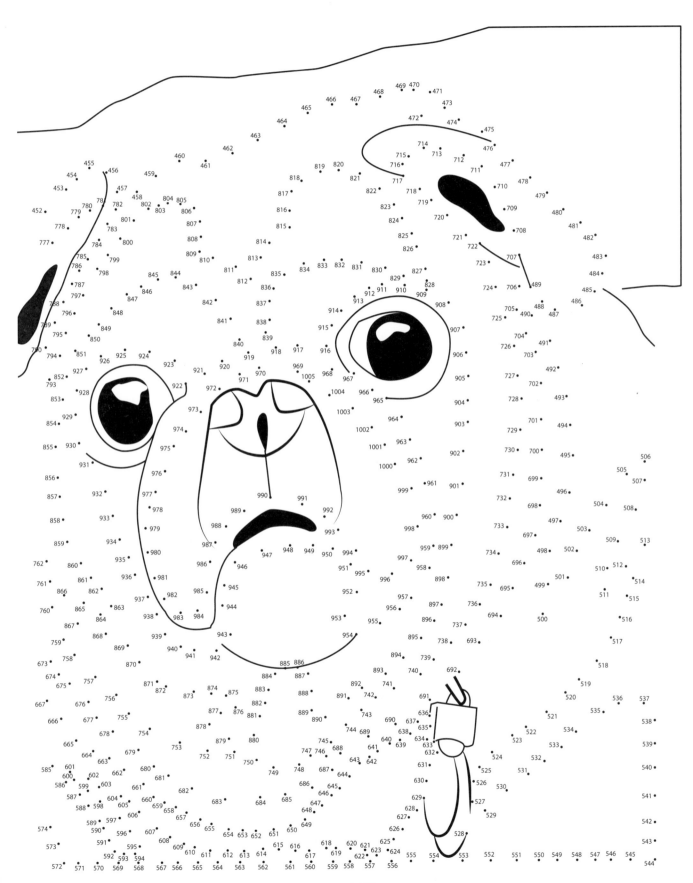

103

Pretty Presentation

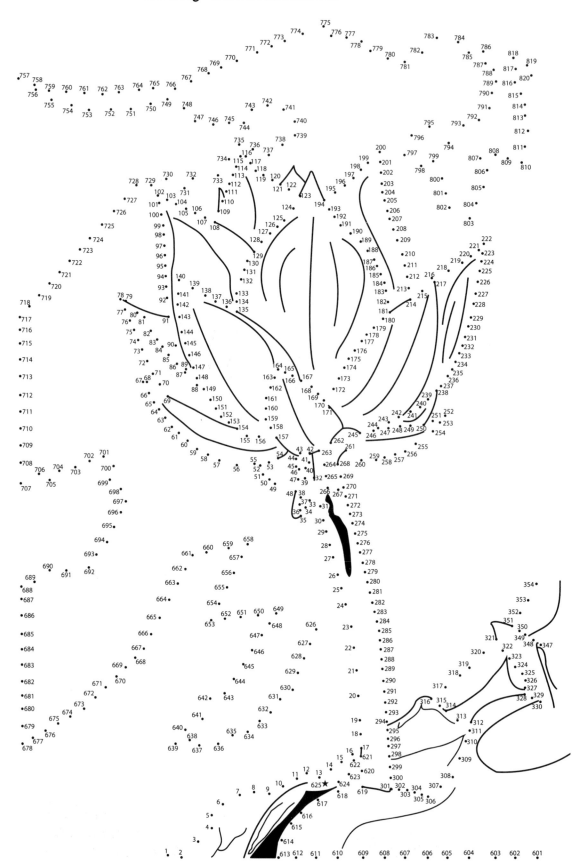

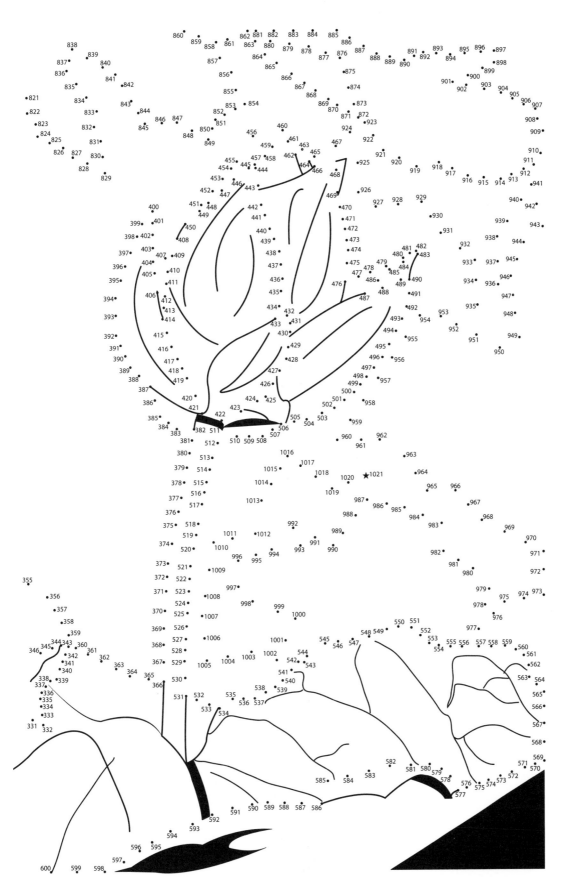

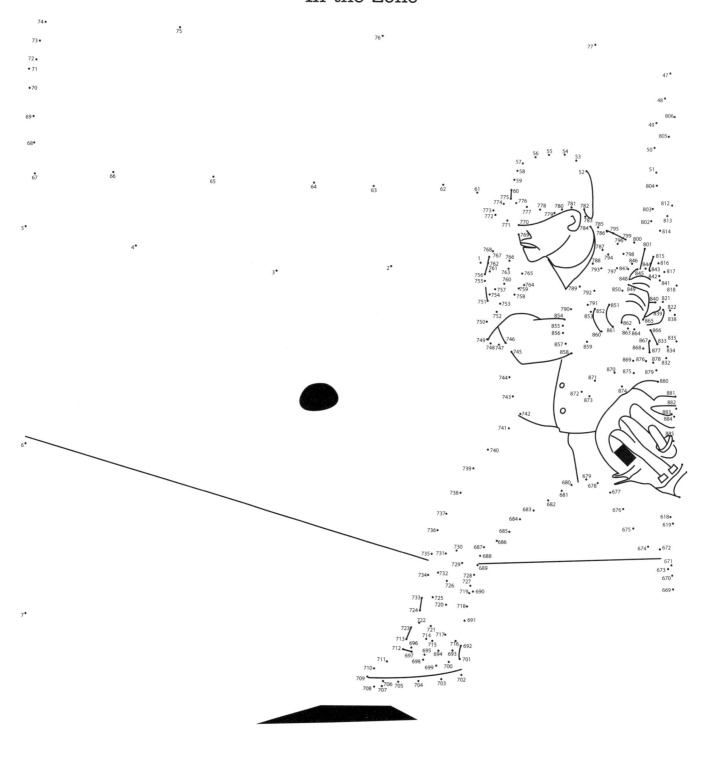

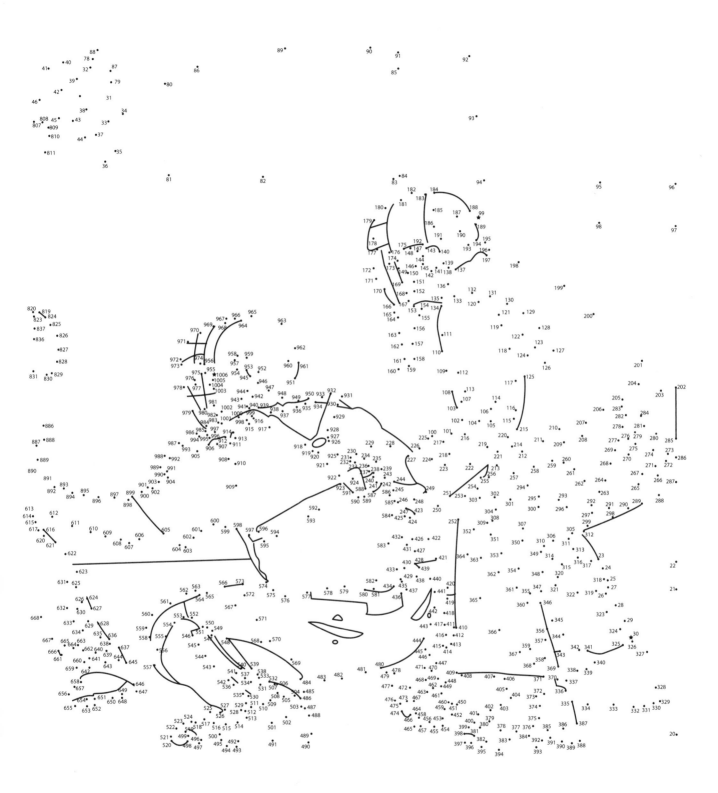

Fleet Feet

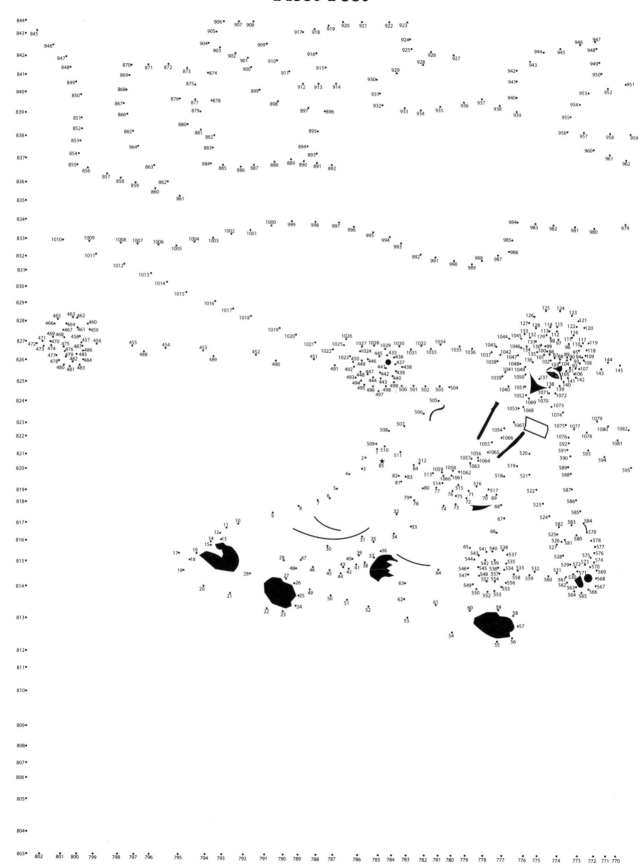

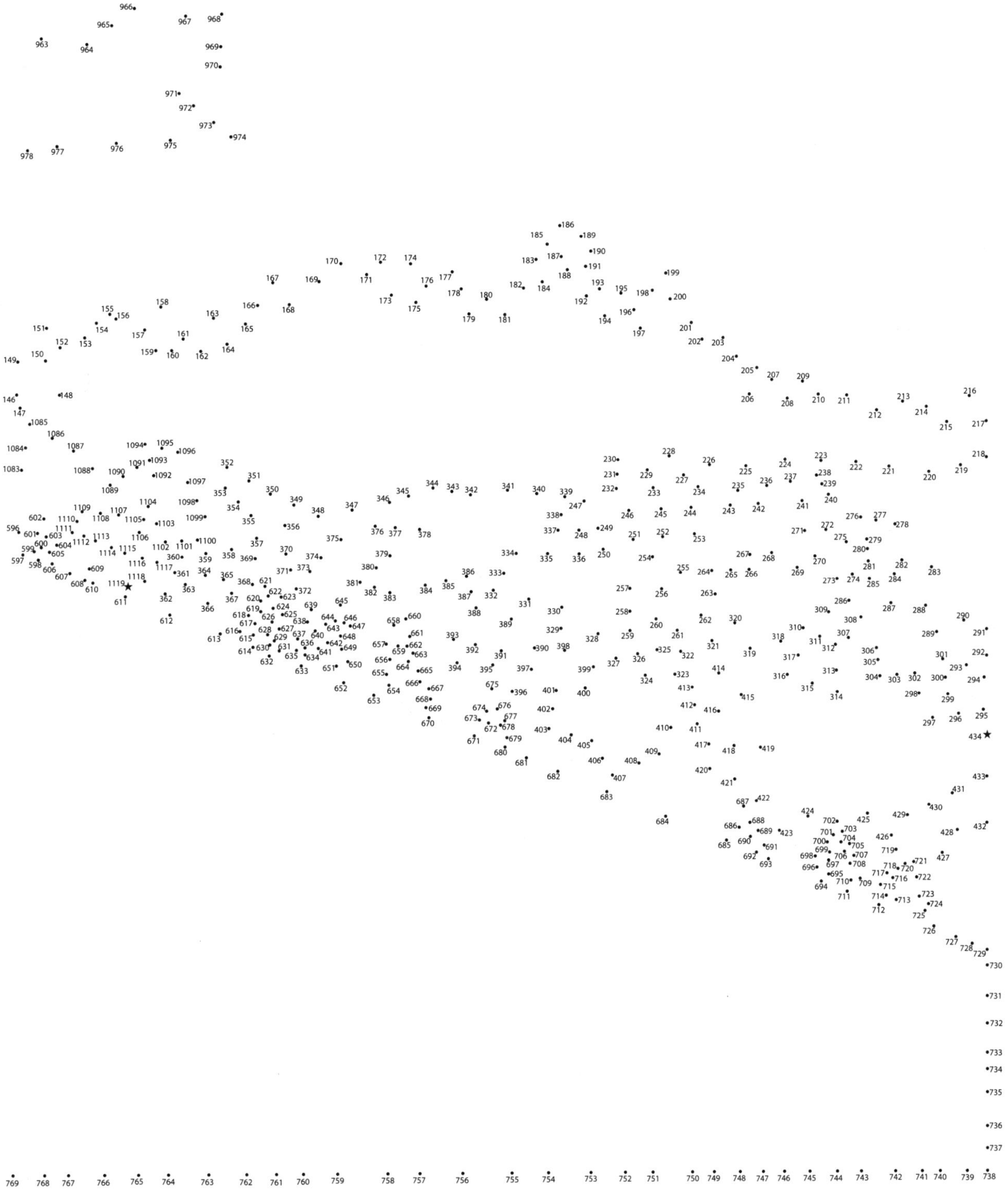

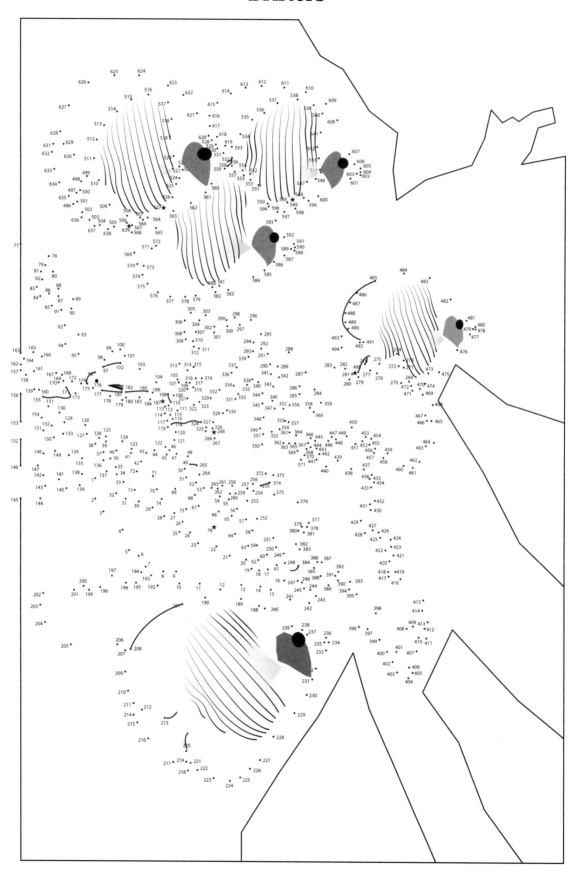

One Passage

111

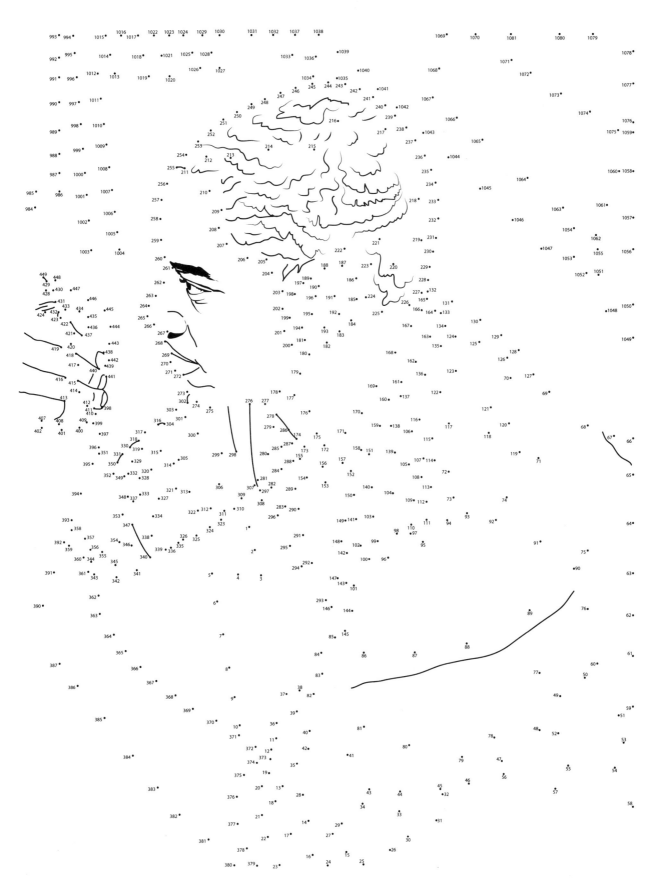

Grace and Power

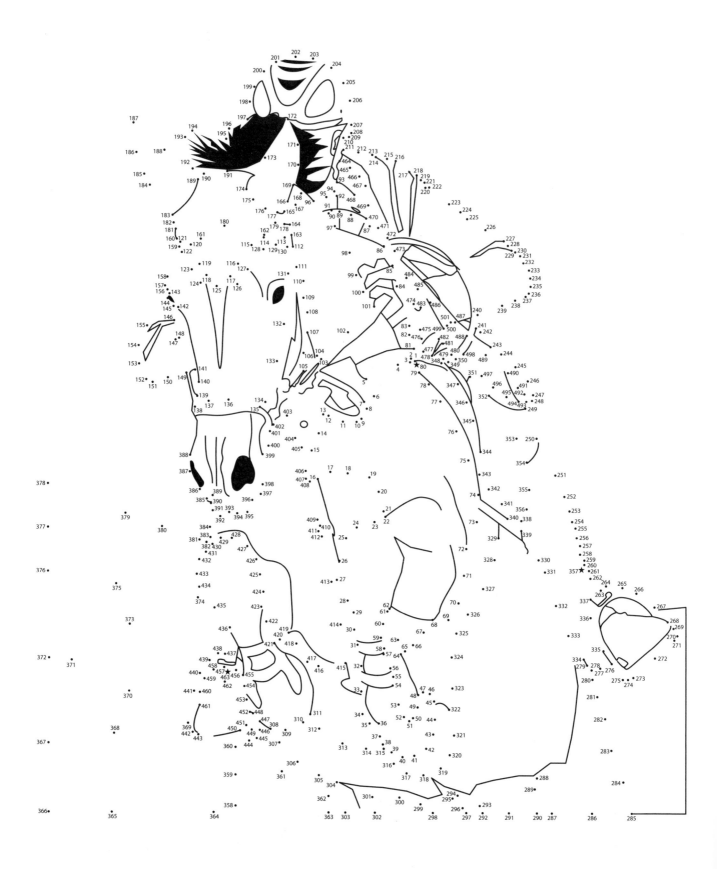

A Bit Jammed

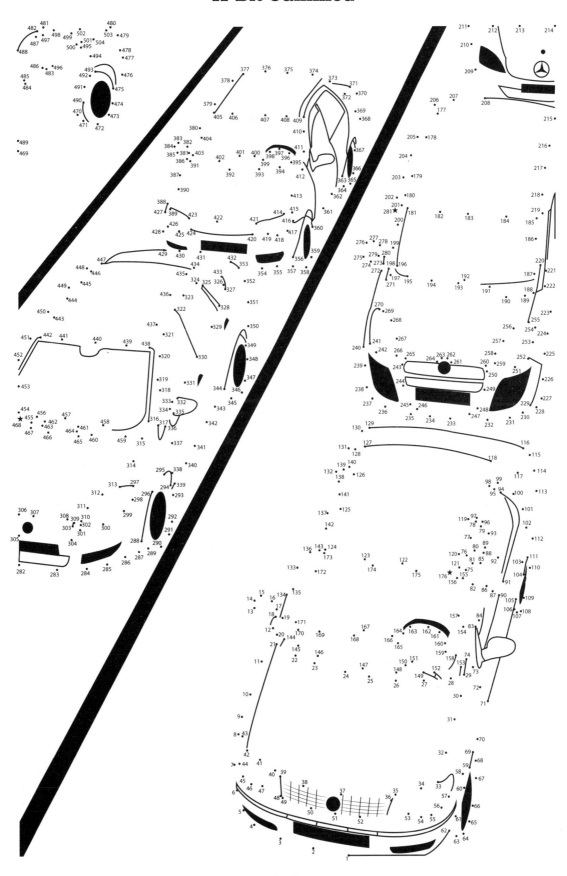

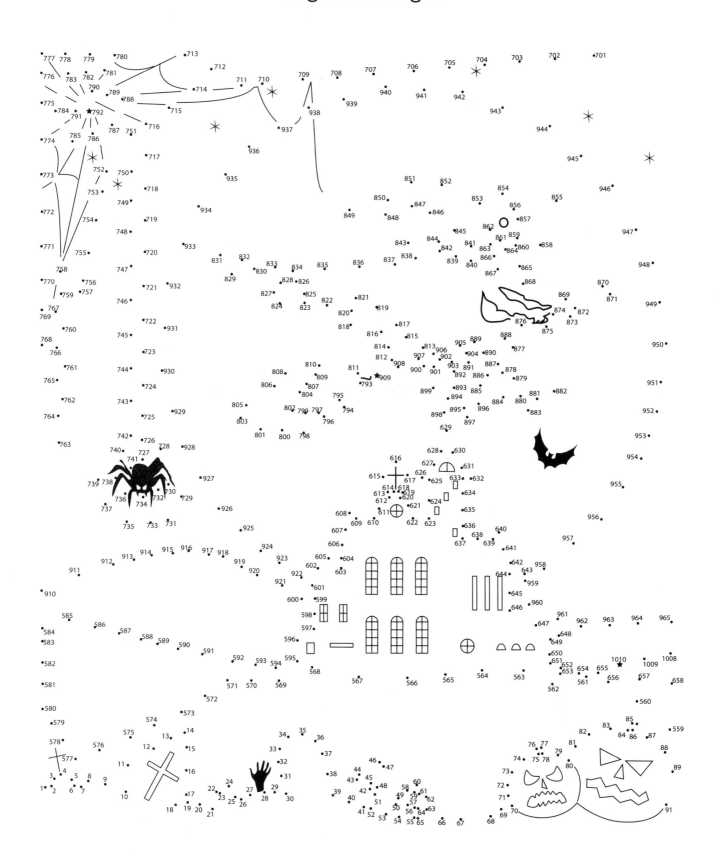

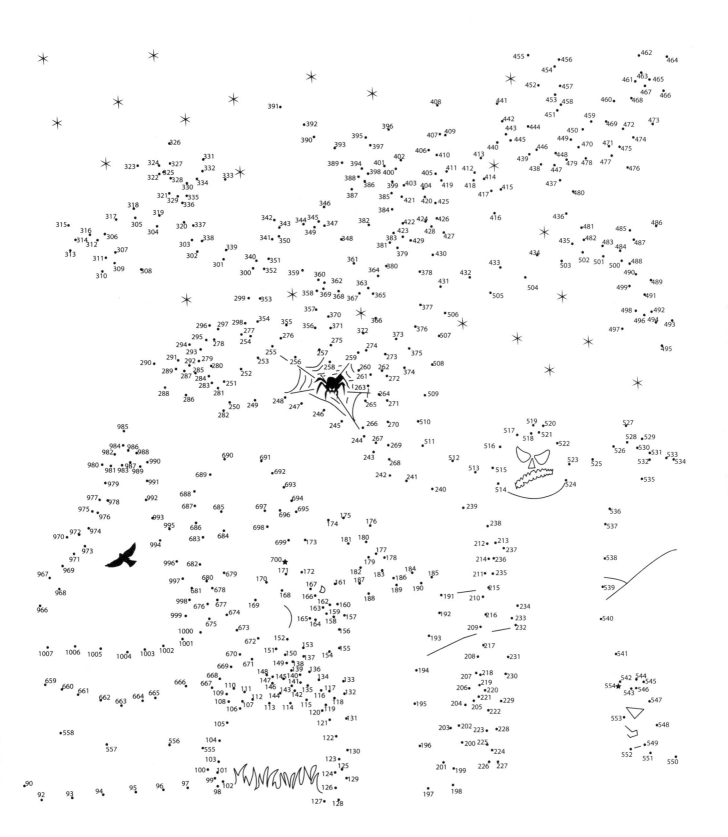

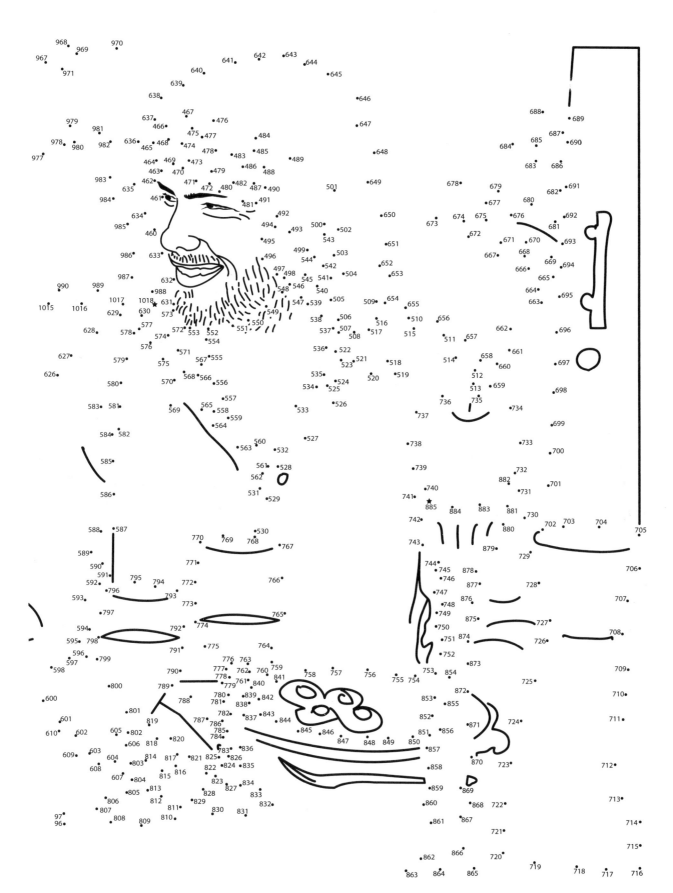

119

Big Bird

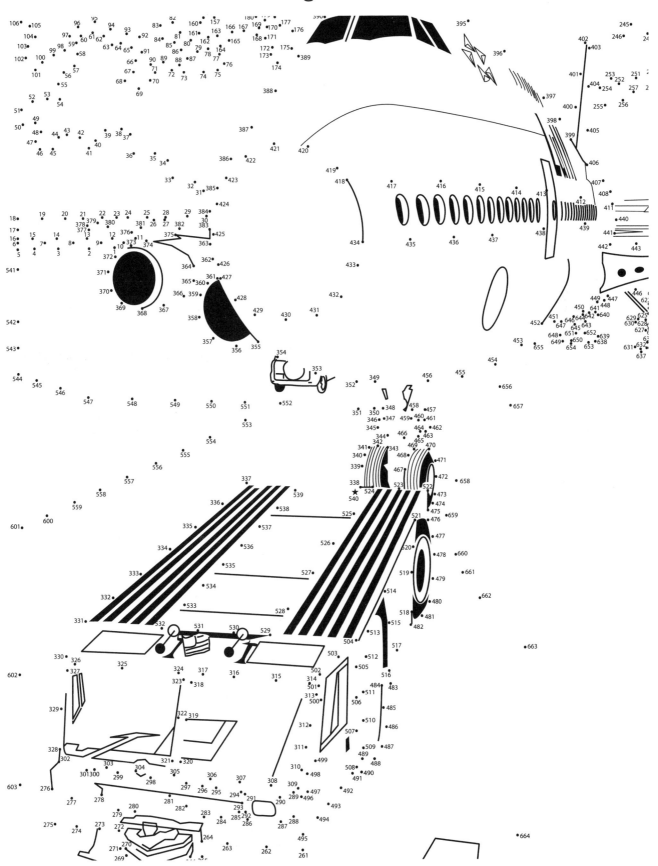

Rope Skills

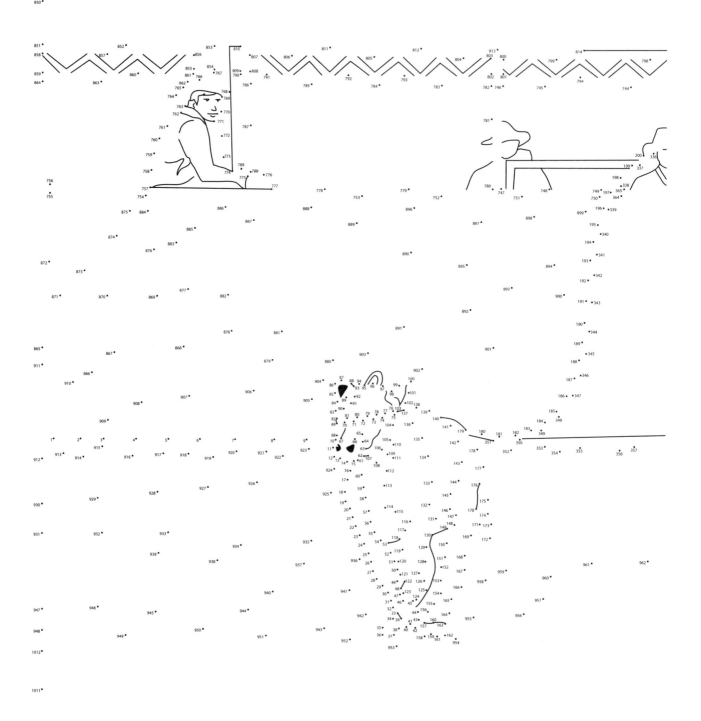

122

Tea or Coffee?

We Winter Here

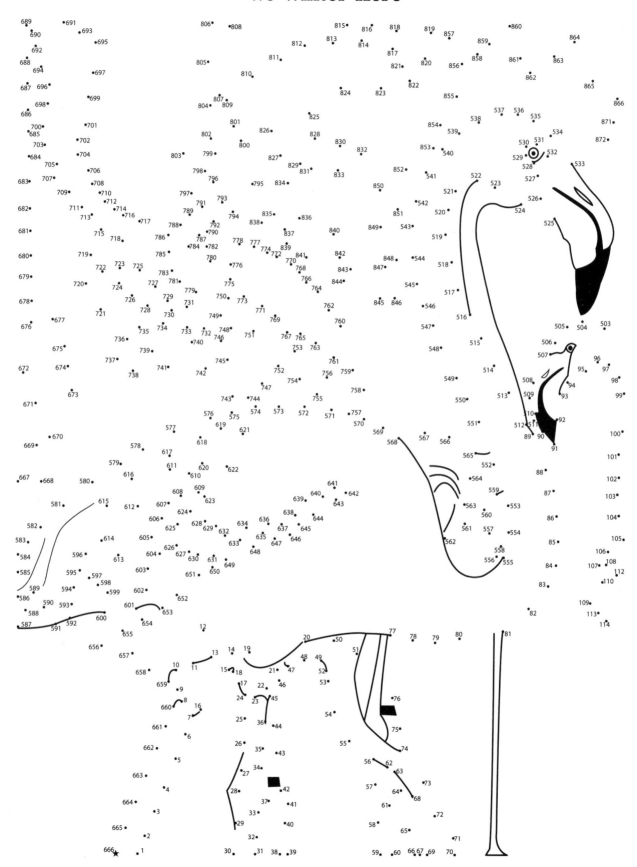

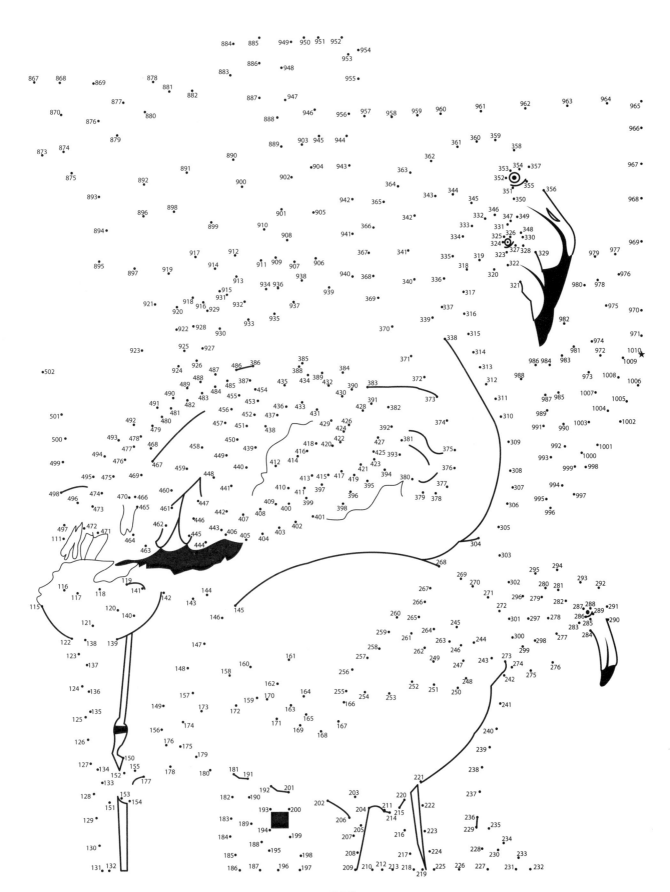

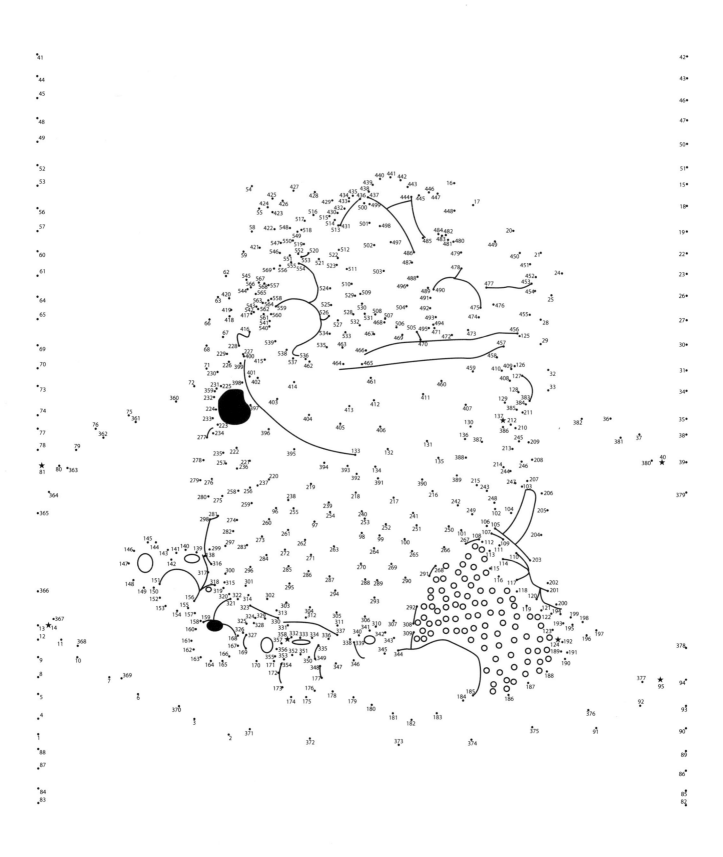

How Many Horses?

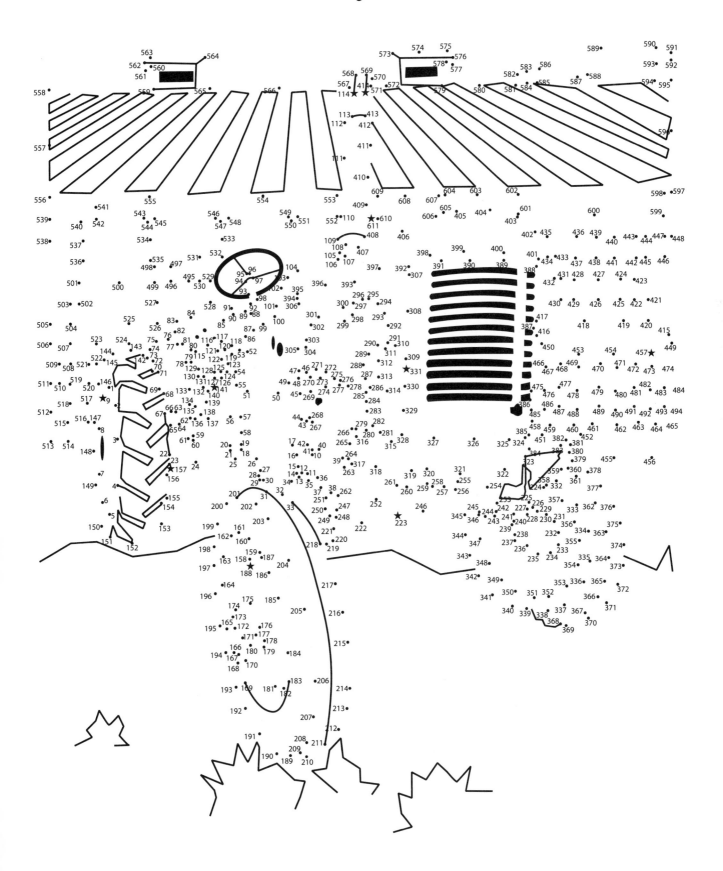

Don't Call Me Spot

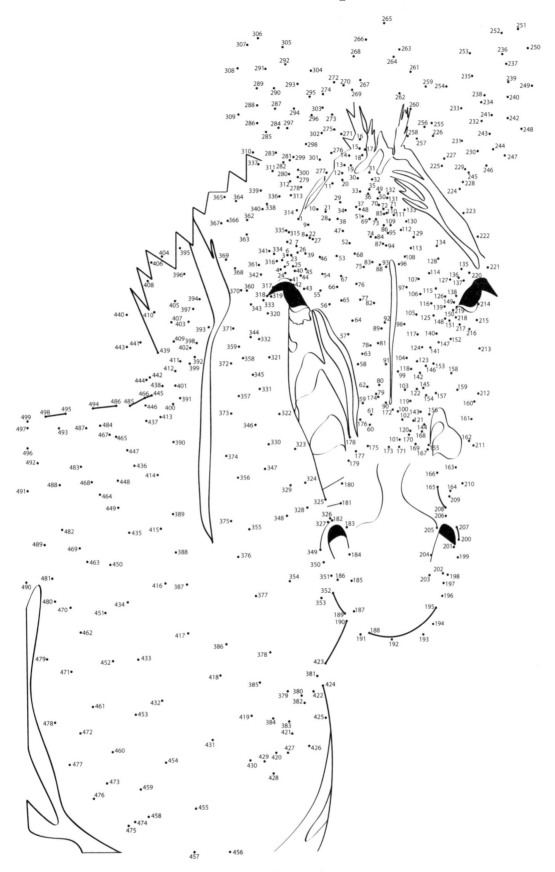

131

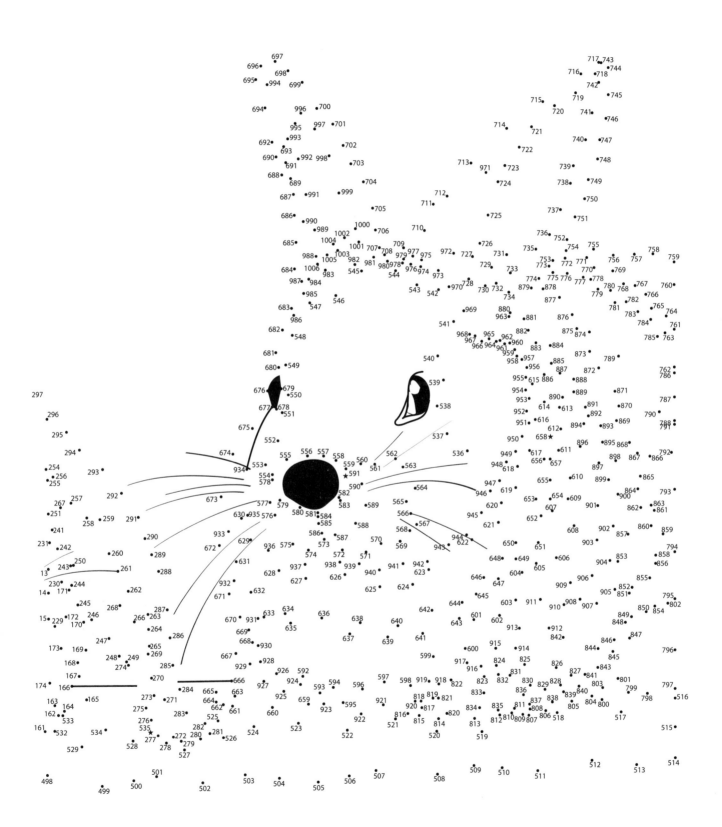

Geared Up

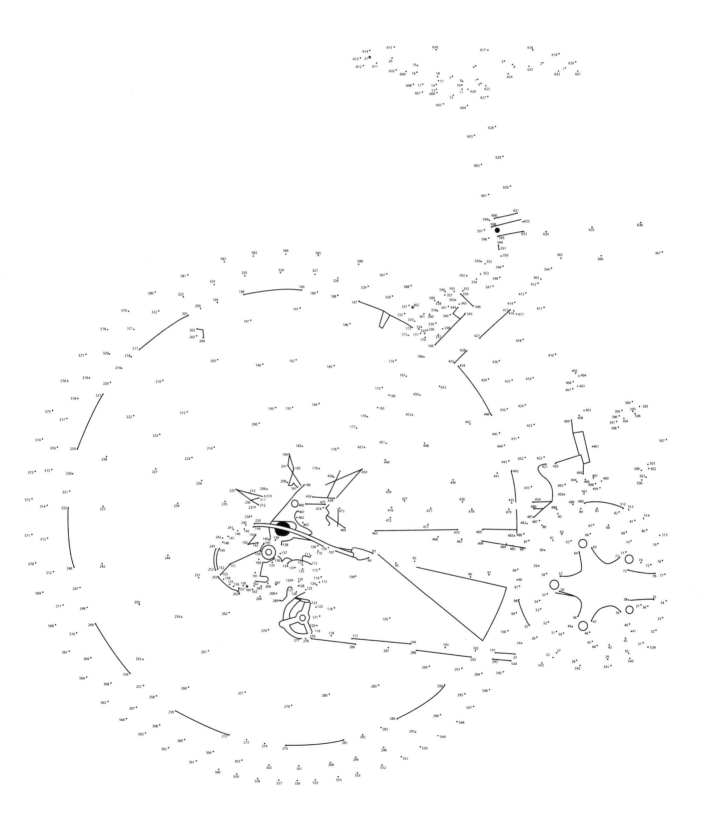

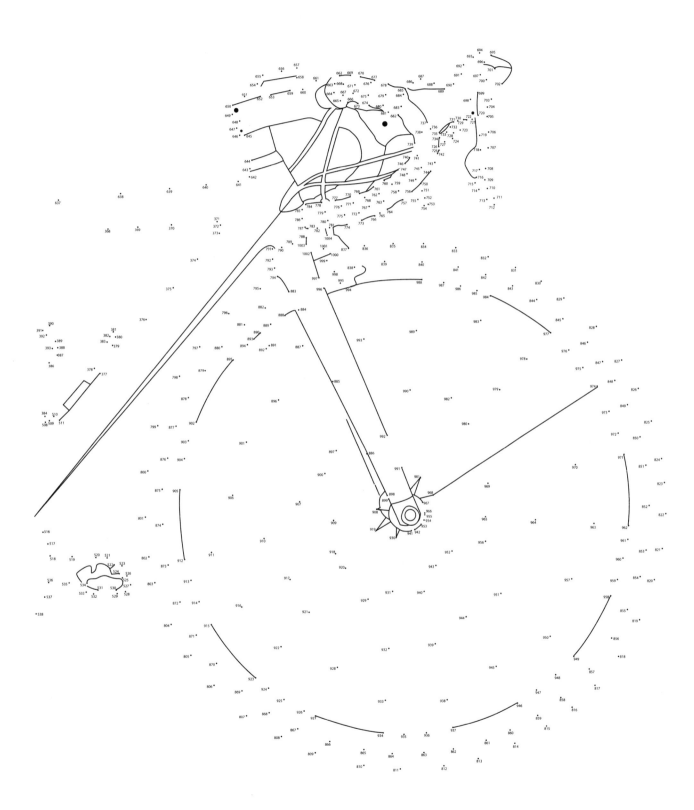

ANSWERS

I'm Not Crabby! (page 4)

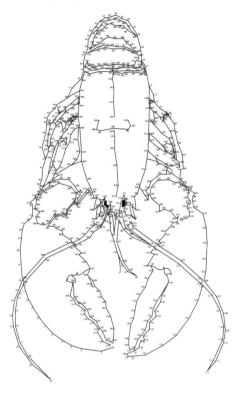

Treats Here (page 5)

We Like Moats (pages 6-7)

Hanging Out (pages 8-9)

ANSWERS

easant Pastime (page 10)

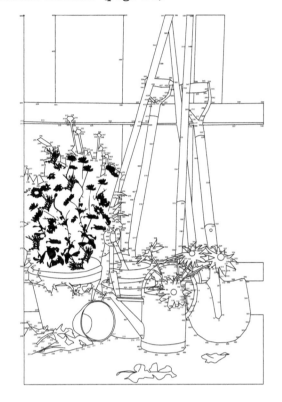

Virtuosity (page 11)

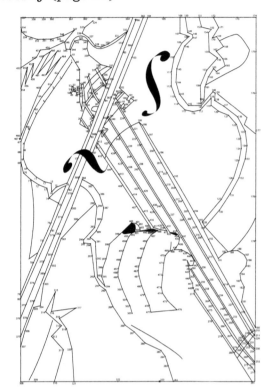

veater Weather (pages 12-13)

Above It All (pages 14-15)

ANSWERS

Timeless (pages 16-17)

Icy Resolve (page 18)

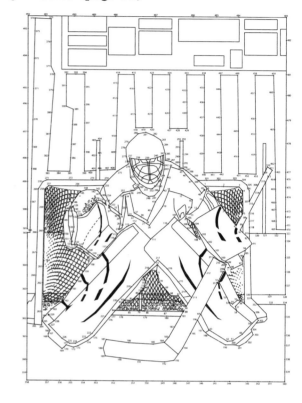

Go Time (page 19)

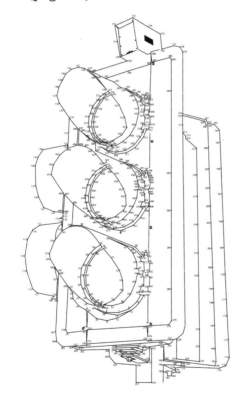

Polar Opposites (pages 20-21)

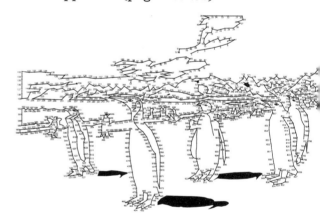

ANSWERS

nced In (pages 22-23)

A Masquerade (pages 24-25)

amond Sight (pages 26-27)

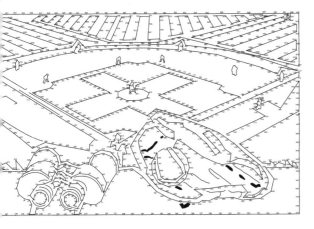

Over the Hump (pages 28-29)

ANSWERS

An Old Mode (page 30)

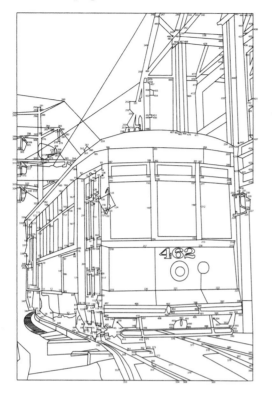

Needed at Night (page 31)

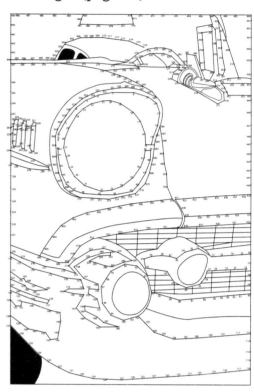

Frozen in Place (pages 32-33)

Got Air? (page 34)

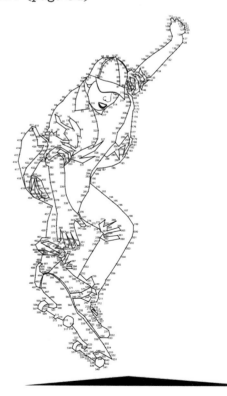

ANSWERS

aboard Sign (page 35)

Perfect Perch (pages 36-37)

In One Sitting (pages 40-41)

Good Return (pages 38-39)

ANSWERS

Smooth and Sunny (pages 42-43)

And Then She Said . . . (pages 44-45)

Hay, But Not a Loft (pages 46-47)

Fruit of the Land (pages 48-49)

ANSWERS

in a Circle (page 50)

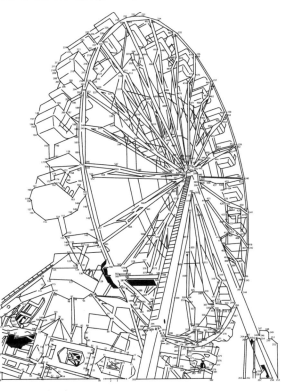

Nectar for Royalty (page 51)

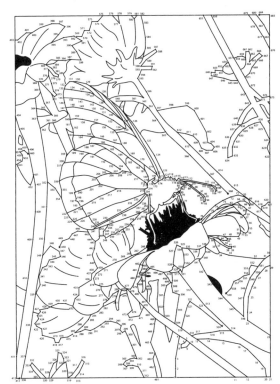

gh Seas (pages 52-53)

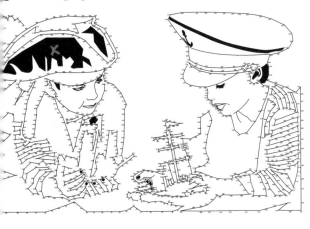

Budding Strategist (page 54)

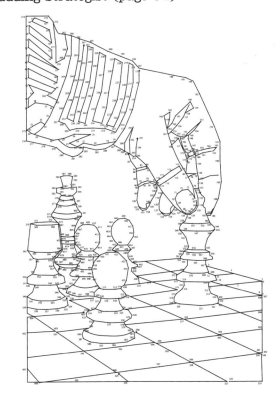

ANSWERS

Prance and Bob (page 55)

A Few Words (pages 56-57)

Implacability (pages 60-61)

Bill Me Later (pages 58-59)

ANSWERS

at's Pretty Wild (page 62)

Serene and Silent (page 63)

p It Off (pages 64-65)

Princess Needed (pages 66-67)

ANSWERS

Greatest of Ease (pages 68-69)

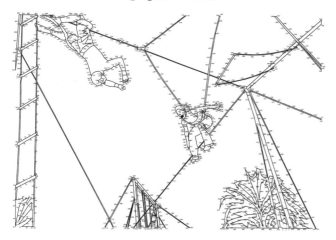

Blown Away (page 70)

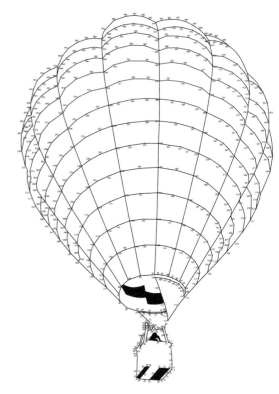

Simple Repast (page 71)

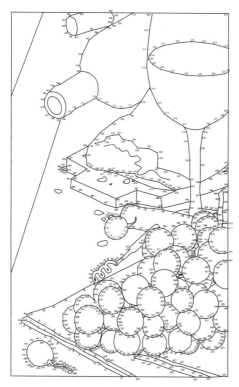

Pride of the Parade (page 72)

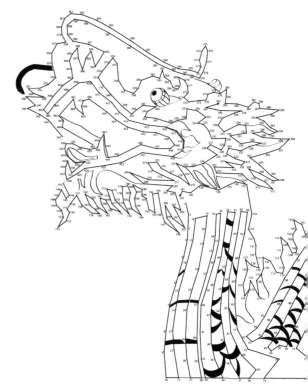

ANSWERS

ll Classic (page 73)

Well Fortified (pages 74-75)

Passed Here (page 77)

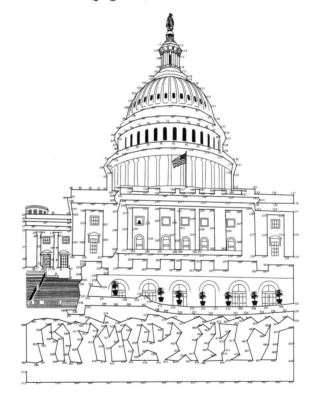

s a Stretch (page 76)

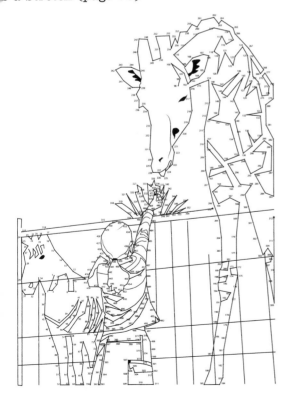

ANSWERS

Sea Sighting (page 78)

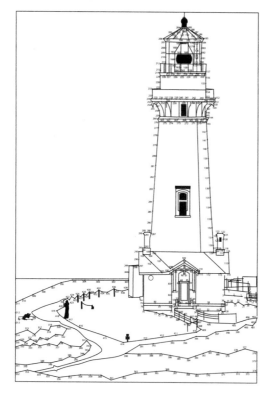

Spotty Coverage (page 79)

Field Work (pages 80-81)

Large Portion (page 82)

ANSWERS

ap One On (page 83)

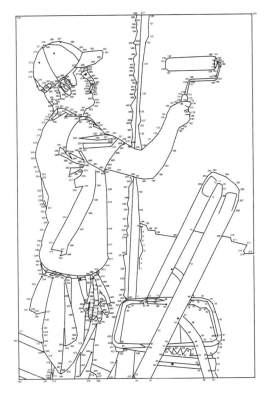

Feeling Winded (pages 84-85)

Raucous Riot (page 87)

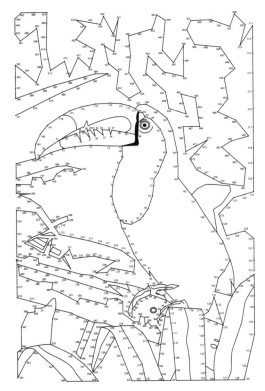

ake Way (page 86)

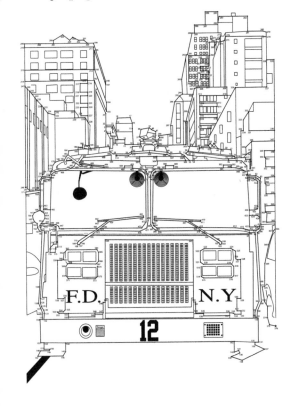

ANSWERS

Western Wear (pages 88-89)

Summer Scene (pages 90-91)

I'm a Night Person (page 92)

City Scene (page 93)

ANSWERS

Steady Hand (page 94)

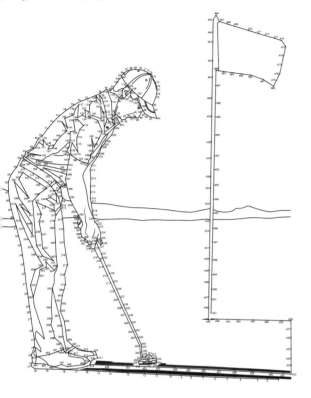

Hang Loose (page 95)

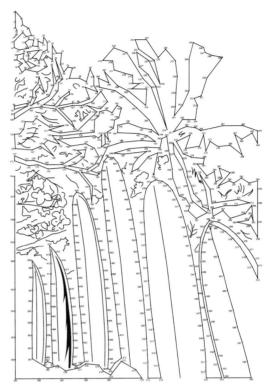

Monumental (page 96)

Wigging Out (page 97)

ANSWERS

Did It! (page 98)

Just Improvise (page 99)

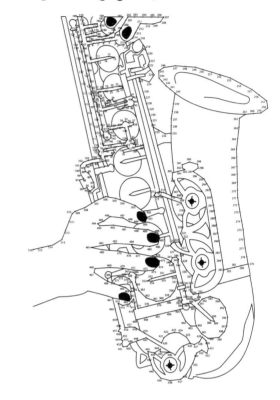

Like Swans (pages 100-101)

What You Lookin' At? (pages 102-103)

ANSWERS

etty Presentation (pages 104-105)

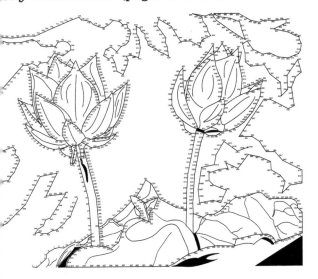

In the Zone (pages 106-107)

eet Feet (pages 108-109)

Drifters (page 110)

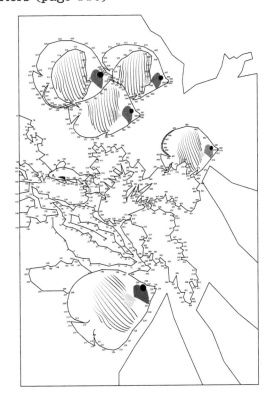

ANSWERS

One Passage (page 111)

We're Armed (pages 112-113)

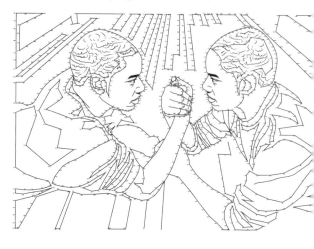

A Bit Jammed (page 115)

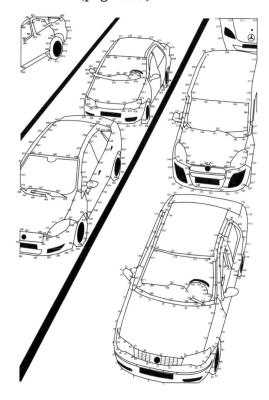

Grace and Power (page 114)

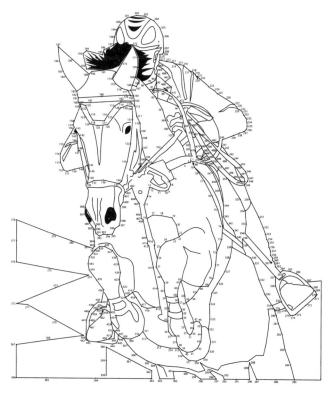

ANSWERS

ght for Fright (pages 116-117)

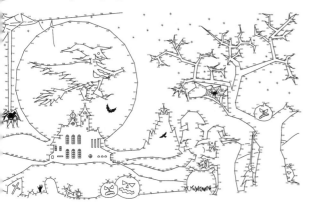

Art of Dining (pages 118-119)

Sound and Sight (page 120)

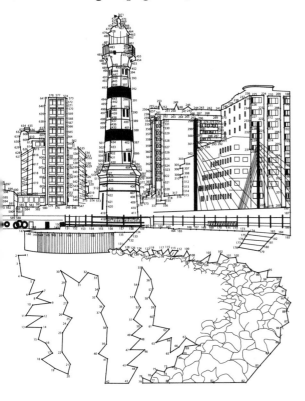

Big Bird (page 121)

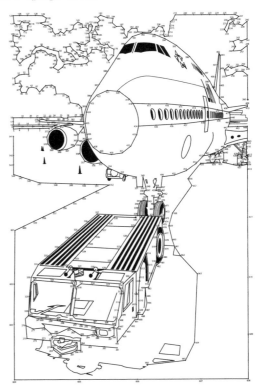

ANSWERS

Rope Skills (pages 122-123)

Tea or Coffee? (pages 124-125)

We Winter Here (pages 126-127)

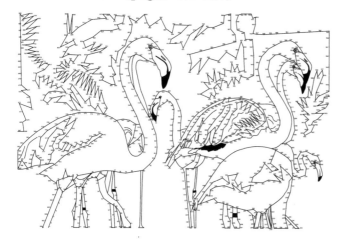

A Big Start (page 128)

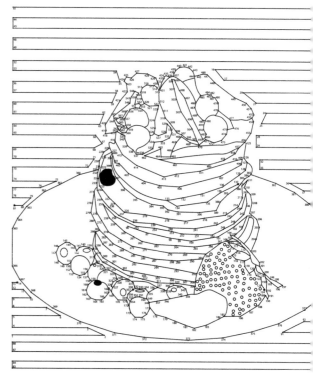

ANSWERS

w Many Horses? (page 129)

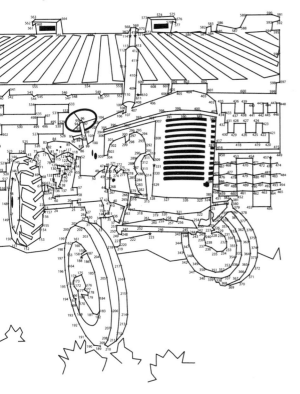

Princely Setting (page 130)

n't Call Me Spot (page 131)

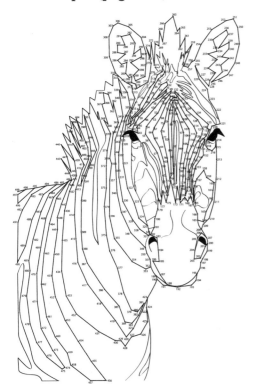

Flighty When Flustered (pages 132-133)

ANSWERS

The Ears Have It (pages 134-135)

Geared Up (pages 136-137)